Leonard William King

Babylonian Religion and Mythology

Leonard William King

Babylonian Religion and Mythology

ISBN/EAN: 9783337182182

Printed in Europe, USA, Canada, Australia, Japan

Cover: Foto ©ninafisch / pixelio.de

More available books at **www.hansebooks.com**

BOOKS ON EGYPT AND CHALDÆA.

By E. A. WALLIS BUDGE, M.A., Litt.D., D.Lit.,
Keeper of the Egyptian and Assyrian Antiquities in
the British Museum,

AND

L. W. KING, M.A.,
Assistant in the Department of Egyptian and Assyrian Antiquities in
the British Museum.

Crown 8vo, 3s. 6d. net each.

Vol. I.—**Egyptian Religion**: Egyptian Ideas of the Future Life. By E. A. Wallis Budge.

Vol. II.—**Egyptian Magic**. By E. A. Wallis Budge.

Vol. III.—**Egyptian Language**: Easy Lessons in Egyptian Hieroglyphics. By E. A. Wallis Budge.

Vol. IV.—**Babylonian Religion**: Babylonian Religion and Mythology. By L. W. King.

The above four Volumes are now ready, and will be followed by others.

LONDON:
KEGAN PAUL, TRENCH, TRÜBNER & CO., Lt.D.
JOHN M. WATKINS, 53, St. Martin's Lane, W.C.

Books on Egypt and Chaldæa

Vol. IV.

BABYLONIAN RELIGION AND MYTHOLOGY

PUBLISHERS' NOTE.

In the year 1894 Dr. Wallis Budge prepared for Messrs. Kegan Paul, Trench, Trübner & Co., Ltd., an elementary work on the Egyptian language, entitled "First Steps in Egyptian," and two years later the companion volume, "An Egyptian Reading Book," with transliterations of all the texts printed in it, and a full vocabulary. The success of these works proved that they had helped to satisfy a want long felt by students of the Egyptian language, and as a similar want existed among students of the languages written in the cuneiform character, Mr. L. W. King, of the British Museum, prepared, on the same lines as the two books mentioned above, an elementary work on the Assyrian and Babylonian languages ("First Steps in Assyrian"), which appeared in 1898. These works, however, dealt mainly with the philological branch of Egyptology and Assyriology, and it was impossible in the space allowed to explain much that needed explanation in the other branches of these subjects—that is to say, matters relating to the archæology, history, religion, etc., of the Egyptians, Assyrians, and Babylonians. In answer to the numerous requests which have been made, a series of short, popular handbooks, on the most important branches of Egyptology and Assyriology has been prepared, and it is hoped that these will serve as introductions to the larger works on these subjects. The present is the fourth volume of the series, and the succeeding volumes will be published at short intervals, and at moderate prices.

Books on Egypt and Chaldæa

BABYLONIAN RELIGION
AND
MYTHOLOGY

BY

L. W. KING, M.A., F.S.A.

ASSISTANT IN THE DEPARTMENT OF EGYPTIAN AND ASSYRIAN ANTIQUITIES,
BRITISH MUSEUM

WITH TWELVE ILLUSTRATIONS

LONDON
KEGAN PAUL, TRENCH, TRÜBNER & CO., Ltd.
PATERNOSTER HOUSE, CHARING CROSS ROAD
1899

PREFACE.

THE object of the present work is to offer to the reader in a handy form an account of the principal facts concerning Babylonian religion and mythology. This account is based upon the cuneiform inscriptions which have been excavated in Mesopotamia during the last fifty-five years, and, as far as possible, the Semitic peoples of the valley of the Tigris and Euphrates have been made to reveal their religious beliefs and superstitions by means of their own writings. Although so much has been done in recent years to explain their religious literature, no finality in the matter must be expected for some time to come, certainly not as long as any important religious text remains unpublished. The fragmentary nature of the available material alone is a great obstacle to the construction of any consecutive narrative, and to the correct grouping of facts, while the renderings of rare Sumerian words and complex ideograms in some cases offer almost insuperable difficulties. Moreover, the variations in the translations made by English and German scholars proclaim the difficulty of the subject, and no systematic and final description of the religion of Babylonia and Assyria is at present possible. In the preparation of this little book the works of the most trustworthy writers on the subject have been diligently consulted, and the translations of cuneiform texts given in the following pages have been specially prepared for the purpose. Every endeavour has also been made to incorporate the results obtained from recently discovered texts, to which in all important cases references are given.

From the facts here printed it is clear that the Babylonians and Assyrians believed in a series of nature gods, and that they had no conception of the existence of one supreme and almighty God. The worship of their gods was tinctured with magic, and many of their prayers and formulæ which they recited during the performance of their religious ceremonies can be regarded as little else than spells, charms, and incantations. Although little by little a higher idea of the majesty of certain gods was developed, and although the Babylonian's conception of a man's duty towards them and towards his neighbour eventually became of a comparatively high moral character, he never succeeded in freeing himself from a belief in the power of magic, sorcery and witchcraft. He attached great importance to the performance of burial ceremonies, imagining that his arrival in the next world depended absolutely upon them; but the life which he believed the soul would lead after death in the underworld seems to have been of a peculiarly joyless character.

Owing to want of space no attempt has been made to discuss from a comparative point of view the legends of the cosmogony and the deluge written in cuneiform, and only the most obvious parallels between parts of them and certain chapters of Genesis have been drawn. It was unnecessary to treat the subject exhaustively, as it is now generally admitted by scholars that the writers of the Pentateuch drew upon the traditions of Babylonia for a number of the statements made in the early chapters of Genesis.

I take this opportunity of expressing my indebtedness to the works of Delitzsch, Jensen, Gunkel, Zimmern, Jeremias, Jastrow, and others, and of thanking Dr. Wallis Budge for his great help in the preparation of the work.

L. W. KING.

LONDON,
October 7th, 1899.

CONTENTS.

CHAPTER		PAGE
I.	The Gods of Babylon	1
II.	Heaven, Earth, and Hell	27
III.	The Legends of Creation	53
IV.	The Story of the Deluge	121
V.	Tales of Gods and Heroes	146
VI.	The Duty of Man to his God and to his Neighbour	200

LIST OF ILLUSTRATIONS.

CHAPTER		PAGE
I.	The Moon-God	15
	The Sun-God	19
II.	The Eastern Door of Heaven	32
	The Gods of the Underworld	39
III.	The Fight between Marduk and Tiāmat	75, 102
	Scene beside a Sacred Tree	113
IV.	A Babylonian Ship	131
V.	Gilgamesh and Ea-bani	162
	Crossing the Waters of Death	170
	The Goddess Ishtar	182
	The South-West Wind	189
VI.	A Babylonian Demon	203

BABYLONIAN RELIGION AND MYTHOLOGY.

CHAPTER I.

THE GODS OF BABYLON.

It was at one time the fashion with many scholars to regard the civilization of the Babylonians as of a purely Semitic origin; and more than one writer on the religion of that country has moulded his work on the fundamental thesis that the Semitic Babylonians and they alone were the originators of the complicated system of religious practise and belief which we know existed from a very early period upon the banks of the Euphrates. Recent excavations in Babylonia, however, have proved one fact with absolute certainty—that before the Semites ever reached Babylonia a non-Semitic race occupied the country, tilled the land, tended herds of cattle, built cities, dug canals, and advanced to a state of considerable civilization. But there are indications that even this race, the Sumerians[1] as they are called, were not the first possessors of the land. It is probable that they themselves were settlers like the Semites of a later time, and that they reached the fertile valley of the rivers from some mountainous home in the northern half of Central Asia. Who occupied the country before the Sumerians came we cannot say, for of the aboriginal inhabitants of the land we know nothing. The first inhabitants of Babylonia of whom we have definite knowledge are the Sumerians; and during recent years our knowledge of them has been vastly increased. In any treatment of the religious beliefs of the Semitic Babylonians, the existence of the Sumerians cannot be ignored, for they profoundly influenced the faith of the Semitic invaders before whose onslaught their empire fell. The religious beliefs of the Babylonians cannot be rightly understood unless at the outset this foreign influence is duly recognized.

To what date we are to assign the beginning of Sumerian influence in Babylonia it is quite impossible to say, though such a date as six or seven thousand years before Christ is not an extravagant estimate for the foundation of the earliest religious centres[2] in the country. The decline of the political power of the Sumerians, on

---

[1] The Sumerians take their name from "Shumēru," an ancient name for Southern Babylonia.

[2] *E.g.*, Nippur, Ur, Shirpurla, etc.

the other hand, may be assigned approximately to the period which lies between B.C. 2500 and B.C. 2300. At the latter date Babylon had been raised to a position of pre-eminence among the cities of the land, and the Semitic population in the country had gained a complete ascendancy over their ancient rivals, whom they gradually absorbed; from this time onwards the city of Babylon maintained her position and never ceased to be the capital of the country to which in later times she gave her name. But in spite of the early date to which we must put back the beginnings of Babylonian civilization, it is only among the remains of a very much later period that we find adequate materials for the study of the Babylonian religion. It is true that during the long course of the history of that country and of Assyria we get occasional glimpses of the religious beliefs and legends, which were current at different periods, from the historical and votive inscriptions of kings and governors. But it is only at quite a late date, that is to say a few years before the fall of Nineveh, that we gain a comparatively full knowledge of Babylonian mythology and belief.

The great religious works of the Babylonians are known to us from documents which do not date from an earlier period than the seventh century B.C. In the palaces that were unearthed at Kuyunjik, the site of Nineveh, there were found, scattered through the mounds of earth, thousands of clay tablets written in the Assyrian character, and in many cases with colophons bearing the name of Ashur-bāni-pal and the statement that he had caused them to be included in his library. This monarch reigned from B.C. 669 to about B.C. 625, and, though one of the last kings to occupy the Assyrian throne, he made strenuous efforts to preserve the ancient literature of Babylonia and Assyria. His scribes visited specially the ancient cities and temples in the south, and made copies of literary compositions of all classes which they found there. These they collected and arranged in his palace at Nineveh, and it is from them that the greater part of our knowledge of Babylonian mythology and religion is derived.

Though the tablets date from the seventh century only, it is possible that the texts inscribed upon them had their origin in a very remote period, and a detailed study of them proves that such was the case. If, for instance, two or more copies of a text are found to differ greatly in detail from one another, we naturally assume that a considerable period has elapsed for such variations to have crept into the text. Besides this, the imperfect condition of many of the originals from which the scribes made their copies, the notes and colophons they added to the texts, and the lists and commentaries they compiled to explain them, prove the antiquity of the literature they studied. Such evidence is conclusive that the religious literature the Assyrians have left us was not of their own production, but was their inheritance from an earlier time. While the Babylonians in their religious beliefs were profoundly influenced by the Sumerians, they in their turn exercised an even greater influence on the Assyrians. The latter people, at first but a handful of colonists from Babylonia, took with them the faith of their mother country, and, though they subsequently gained their independence, and after many centuries of conflict held the elder branch of their race in subjection, their system of religion, with but few changes and modifications, was Babylonian to the core. Hence their religious works and writings may be used as material for the study of the Babylonian religion.

When we examine these Assyrian tablets, and attempt to gain from them a knowledge of the gods of Babylon, we find they present us with a truly bewildering number of deities. The Babylonians and Assyrians were a conservative people, and the priestly class, to whose labours we are indebted for our knowledge of the Babylonian religion, faithfully collected and chronicled all local traditions and beliefs, no matter whence they came. Their religion was still a living thing, and they had not lost belief in the existence or the power of the gods, but they studied their national traditions to some extent from their literary side; and they sought to classify and arrange into some system the numerous and sometimes conflicting traditions which had arisen and obtained currency at different periods in quite different parts of the country. The largest tablet that has been recovered from Ashur-bāni-pal's library, for instance, is inscribed with a list of the names of the gods and their titles. The tablet when complete must have measured some 11 × 16 inches; it was inscribed on each side with six columns of minute writing, every column containing over one hundred and fifty lines, and nearly every line giving the name of a separate deity.[1] This is only one out of many tablets inscribed with lists of the names of the gods, and the existence of these documents serves to show that in the literature of the period we must expect to find the Babylonian religion in a fully advanced state of its development.

Were we entirely dependent on such lists and catalogues it would be hard to gather a very consistent or very intelligible notion of what the Babylonian gods were like; but fortunately this is not the case. Numbers of hymns and prayers have been recovered, which, by the titles and attributes therein ascribed to the gods, enable us to trace their relationships to one another and their respective rank and power. Stories and legends of the gods have also been preserved, and from these it is possible to construct a fairly complete sketch of Babylonian mythology. Moreover, the names of the gods frequently figure in the historical inscriptions

---

[1] The tablet is exhibited in the British Museum, Nineveh Gallery, Case I., No. 4.

of Babylonian and Assyrian kings, not only of this late period, but also in those of rulers who occupied the throne during many earlier periods of the country's history. The victories gained over enemies were ascribed by each ruler to the help vouchsafed him by his own gods, and from the names of those he mentions we learn what gods were held in special reverence during his reign. The kings of Babylon, too, were great builders and delighted to construct new temples and to restore the old ones which had fallen into decay. From the records of their building operations, and from the votive tablets deposited in the temples, we gain much information regarding the worship of the deities in whose honour they were made. Another source of information, especially for the early Sumerian period, are the lists of temple revenues and accounts; while the very names of private persons preserved in business documents of various dates, containing as so many of them do the names of gods, serve to indicate roughly the changes which the principal gods experienced in the popular estimation. It is of course to be regretted that we do not possess copies of the great religious and mythological works of the Babylonians during the earlier periods of their history, from which it would be possible to trace with absolute certainty the course of their religious development. The numerous indirect sources of information referred to, however, enable us to control and classify the religious literature of the later Assyrian and Babylonian empires. By these means it is possible to gain a knowledge from native sources of Babylonian mythology and belief, and to supplement the scanty references to the religion of the country which are found in the Old Testament and in the works of the classical writers.

The gods of the Babylonians, in the forms under which they were worshipped during the later historical periods, were conceived as beings with very definite and characteristic personalities. All the great gods, while wielding superhuman powers, were regarded as endowed with human forms, and, though they were not visible, except in dreams and visions, to their worshippers, each was thought to possess a definite character and to have a body and features peculiar to himself. Not only were they like unto men in body, but in thought and feeling they were also very human. Like men they were born into the world, and like men they loved and fought, and even died. The Babylonians, in fact, had a very material conception of the higher powers. They had no belief in a supreme and abstract deity of a different mould and nature to themselves; and though they ascribed all power and might to many of the greater gods they worshipped, they pictured these beings as swayed by human passions, and as acting in dependence on each other. About their gods they composed strange tales and legends, in which we read how some of them performed acts of bravery and valour, how others displayed cunning and treachery, and how others again exhibited fear and greed. It is true that, unlike men, their power was unlimited, they wielded magical weapons, and uttered spells and words of power; but for all that they were fashioned in human mould; the separation between the Babylonian and his god was not in nature but in degree.

In following the doings of the gods and in noting the attributes ascribed to them, we are naturally confronted by the problem as to what suggested to the Babylonian his precise differentiation in their characters. Was it merely fancy or arbitrary invention on his part? We need not appeal to the comparative study of religion to answer the question in the negative, for the characters of the gods themselves betray their origin. They are personifications of natural forces; in other words, the gods and many of the stories told concerning them are the best explanation the Babylonian could give, after many centuries of observation, of the forces and changes he saw at work around him in the natural world. He saw the sun pass daily overhead, he observed the phases of the moon and the motions of the stars; he felt the wind and feared the tempest; but he had no notion that these things were the result of natural laws. In company with other primitive peoples he explained them as the work of beings very like himself. He thought of nature as animated throughout by numberless beings, some hostile and some favourable to mankind, in accordance with the treatment he had experienced from them. From the greater powers and forces in nature he deduced the existence of the greater gods, and in many of the legends and myths he told concerning them we may see his naïve explanation of the working of the universe. He did not speak in allegory or symbol, but believed his stories literally, and moulded his life in accordance with their teaching.

Babylonian religion, therefore, in its general aspect may be regarded as a worship of nature, and the gods themselves may be classified as the personifications of various natural powers. But here at the outset we meet with a difficulty which has not yet been quite satisfactorily explained. During its early history the country was not a corporate whole under one administration, but the great cities, with the land immediately adjacent to them, formed a number of independent states. It was only after many centuries of separate existence, or of temporary coalition, that a permanent fusion was brought about between these separate kingdoms. Back in this dim past we can trace the existence of many of the great Babylonian gods of later times, and, as in later times, so still more at this early period, we find their worship was not equally prevalent throughout the country, but the cult of each deity was specialized and centred in separate cities. Enlil, the god of the earth, for instance, was worshipped in the earliest period at Nippur; Ea, the god of the deep, at Eridu; Nannar, the Moon-god, at Ur; Utu, the Sun-god, at Larsa, and so on. Now taken in the aggregate, the worship of all these deities presents a consistent picture of the worship of nature in its different parts, and for the later periods such a picture no doubt accurately corresponds to the general character of the national religion. But in the earliest period the great cities of the land were not parts of a single kingdom; and it is not quite clear how this local distribution of the great natural gods among a number of originally independent cities can be explained.

In seeking a solution of this problem it is necessary to realize the fact that the religious system of the Babylonians was the product of a long period of gradual development. The consistent scheme of nature worship practised by the later Babylonians was not received by them in a complete and finished form from their remote ancestors and predecessors in the land. At this remote period we may assume that its state was a very simple and a very primitive one. The horizon of these early peoples embraced little more than the walls of the cities in which they dwelt, and each city was content to worship and do battle for the honour of its local god; the fortune of the god was bound up with that of the city, and the downfall of the god followed close on the ruin of the city. With the gradual amalgamation of these separate cities into larger states, an adjustment between the local gods was necessary. In any such coalition the god of the predominant city would naturally take precedence over those of the conquered or dependent cities with which he became associated. It is conceivable that in this way the relationships between some of the gods of the Babylonians arose. Even so, it is difficult to trace the process by which a local city-god became associated with one of the great powers of nature, and to decide whether his aspect as a god of a special department of the universe was inherent in his nature from the beginning, or was due to some subsequent development. Such questions present a number of attractive problems, many of which will doubtless be solved as more material relating to the earliest period of Babylonian history is published. Meanwhile, in whatever way we may explain it, the local worship in different cities of Babylonia of many of the greater natural gods is one of the most striking characteristics of the Babylonian system.

In giving a sketch of the principal gods of Babylonia it will be expedient to confine ourselves in the main to the periods of Babylonian history subsequent to the rise of the city of Babylon to power, which was followed by the consolidation of the separate portions of the country into a single state. It would of course be possible to push our enquiry back into the earliest period when the Sumerian was in possession of the

SUMERIAN AND SEMITIC DEITIES. 13

country and the influence of the Semite was still unfelt. Although the study of the Sumerian deities is still in its infancy, it would be possible to give their names as found in the early inscriptions from Niffer, Muḳayyar and Tell Loh, and, with the help of the later explanatory lists of the Assyrians, to trace in some measure their adoption and the modification of their names, attributes, etc., by the Babylonians.[1] But to follow such a plan within the limits of the present volume would result in little more than a catalogue of names and equations, many of which are still matters of conjecture. It will be better therefore to treat only of those great Semitic deities who figure so prominently in Babylonian mythology, and to refer to their Sumerian prototypes only in so far as they illustrate their later characters.

Even during the Semitic period the Babylonian company of the gods underwent considerable changes. The assimilation of the Sumerian deities was not a sudden process, and the meeting of the two systems did not produce uniform results throughout the country. Moreover, in the later as in the earlier periods, every city had its own local god, to whose service the whole city was devoted, and around whose temple local traditions and local myths gathered and flourished. The prominence which any one such local tradition attained in the Babylonian system was in proportion to the

[1] See the names and attributes of the various deities collected by Jastrow in his *Religion of Babylonia and Assyria*, pp. 51 ff.

political position and influence of the city in which it arose. It is not a matter of surprise, therefore, that we come across <u>varying traditions</u> with regard to the positions and relationships of some of the gods. But with the gradual unification of the country many such variant traditions were harmonized and explained by the priesthood. It is thus possible, while making full allowance for the influence of local beliefs and of political changes, to give a brief sketch of the company of the Babylonian gods which will harmonize with their position and character in the great religious and mythological and legendary works of the nation.

At the head of the company of the gods may be set the great triad of deities <u>Anu</u>, <u>Bēl</u> and <u>Ea</u>, whose spheres of influence together embraced the entire universe. Anu was the god of heaven, Bēl the god of the earth and of mankind, and Ea the god of the abyss of water beneath the earth. At a very early period in Sumerian history we find these three deities mentioned in close connection with each other under their Sumerian names of Anna (Anu), <u>Enlil</u> (Bēl), and <u>Enki</u> (Ea). Lugalzaggisi, who caused the inscription to be written in which their names occur, was one of the earliest Sumerian rulers of whose reign we have evidence, and we can thus trace back the existence of this great triad of gods to the very beginning of history. During the later periods the connection of these deities with each other, as the three great gods

Copy of an impression from a cylinder-seal. Ur-Gur, King of Ur, about B.C. 2500, performing an act of worship before Enzu, or Sin, the Moon-God. The text reads: "Khashkhamer, thy servant, governor of the town of Ishkun-Sin, [has dedicated this seal on thy behalf], O Ur-Gur, mighty hero, King of Ur." (British Museum, No. 89,126.)

of the universe, remained unshaken. Each member of the triad had his own centre of worship. Thus Anu, though he had temples in other parts of the country, was paid peculiar reverence in Uruk, the Babylonian name of the city of Erech, which is mentioned as one of the oldest cities of Babylonia in the table of nations in Genesis.[1] The god Bêl, as has been already stated, was identified by the Semites with the Sumerian deity Enlil, whose worship in E-kur, his temple in the city of Nippur, was the oldest local cult of which we have evidence in the archaic inscriptions that have yet been recovered. The worship of the third member of the triad, Ea, originated in Eridu, the southernmost of the great cities of Babylonia, the site of which, now marked by the mound of Abu Shahrēn, stands fifty miles from the mouth of the Shaṭṭ el-Arab, but which in the earliest period of Babylonian history, before the formation of the present delta, must have stood on the shore of the Persian Gulf.

After these three deities with their world-wide dominion may be set a second triad, consisting of the two great gods of light, SIN and SHAMASH, and the god of the atmosphere, RAMMĀN. Sin, the Moon-god, identified also with NANNAR, had two centres of worship, the temple E-gish-shir-gal in Ur, and the temple E-khul-khul in Kharran, of which the former was the more ancient. In Ur the worship of the Moon-god

[1] Genesis x. 10.

was celebrated from remote antiquity, and in influence and splendour his cult appears to have eclipsed that of Shamash, the Sun-god, whose worship was centred in the cities of Sippar and Larsa, in two great temples each of which bore the name of E-babbara, "the bright house." According to one tradition Shamash was regarded as the son of the Moon-god, and this subordination of Sun-worship to the cult of the Moon is an interesting peculiarity of early Babylonian religion. At a later period, when the system of mythology was more fully developed, the Sun-god attained a position of greater prominence. He was then regarded as the judge of heaven and earth, and in the legends it was his decision to which appeal was made in cases of wrong and injustice. The god Rammān, while particularly associated with thunder and lightning, was in general the god of the atmosphere and controlled the clouds, the mist and the rain. He was held in especial reverence by the Assyrian kings who loved to compare the advance of their forces in battle to the onslaught of the Storm-god.

The most prominent deity in the company of the Babylonian gods was MARDUK, who, as the local god of Babylon, naturally claimed the highest respect from the men of his own city. The extension of his influence was a result of the rise of Babylon to the position of the capital city in a united empire, and it is to this fact we may trace his identification with the old

Scene from the so-called "Sun-god Tablet." Nabû-pal-iddina, king of Babylon, about B.C. 900, performing an act of worship before Shamash, the Sun-god, who is seated within his shrine in the temple of Sippar. (British Museum, No. 12,137.)

Babylonian deity Bēl, whose worship had flourished for so many centuries at Nippur, and the prominent part which he plays in Babylonian legend and mythology. From the days of Khammurabi onward Marduk never lost this position of supremacy among the other gods. Traces of his original subordinate character at the time when Babylon was still unknown may be seen in the fact that he was never regarded as the oldest of the gods, nor as endowed from the beginning with his later attributes; he was conceived as having won his power and supremacy by his own valour and by the services he rendered both to gods and to mankind. In intimate association with Marduk may be mentioned NABŪ, the god of Borsippa, a city which is marked to-day by the mound of Birs Nimrūd,[1] and which, built a little to the south-west of Babylon on the opposite bank of the Euphrates, was in its later period little more than a suburb of the capital. To this fact we may trace the close connection of Nabū with Marduk, whose son and minister he was supposed to have been. E-zida, his temple in Borsippa, was closely associated with E-sagil, Marduk's great shrine in Babylon, and these two sanctuaries were the most famous in the country.

Another prominent deity was NERGAL, whose temple, E-shidlam, in the city of Kūtū, or Cuthah, was one

[1] A place situated about two hours' ride from the modern city of Hillah.

of the oldest and largest sanctuaries in Northern Babylonia. In general character Nergal was the god of battle, and, no doubt from its destructive nature, of pestilence also; in still another capacity he was regarded as the god of the dead.[1] The connection of Nergal with the city of Cuthah was never severed throughout the long period of Babylonian history. Dungi, one of the earliest kings of the city of Ur, records the building or restoration of his shrine in that city, and more than two thousand years later, among the Babylonians whom Sargon sent to colonize Samaria, we read of certain men of Cuth, or Cuthah, who made an image of Nergal,[2] to whom they trusted to preserve them from the lions that roamed through the devastated land. A god who was in later times closely associated with Nergal is NINIB. The reading of his name is conjectural, and his original character is also a matter of some uncertainty, but under the Assyrian kings his personality was more clearly indicated. By them he was regarded as a god of battle and the chase, and it was to Nergal and Ninib that they ascribed the gift of their mighty weapons. The Fire-god, NUSKU, may also be mentioned among the more important deities, in view of the prominent position he occupies in the magical works of the Babylonians.

The Babylonian goddesses, with one exception, are not very imposing figures, nor are their characters

---

[1] See below, p. 37.   [2] 2 Kings xvii. 30.

very sharply defined or differentiated. Their position corresponded to some extent with the inferior position of women in Babylonia. It has already been remarked that the Babylonian conceived his gods to be very human in their form and feelings, and it was but natural that his picture of their wives should have been drawn after the same model. Their principal functions in fact were to receive the favours of their lords and to become the mothers of a younger generation of gods. In several instances we may trace their position of dependence in the very names by which they were known. Thus ANATU, the wife of Anu, and BĒLIT, the wife of Bēl, in name as well as nature are merely female counterparts of the male deities with whom they are associated. DAMKINA, the wife of Ea, was a slightly more important personage to judge from the numerous hymns addressed to her in the later period, a fact that may perhaps be explained as arising from her position as the mother of Marduk. TSARPANITUM, Marduk's wife, however, was of little account away from her partner, and the same may be said of TASHMETU the wife of Nabū, NINGAL the wife of the Moon-god, AI the wife of the Sun-god, SHALA the wife of Rammān, GULA the wife of Ninib, and LAZ the wife of Nergal. In fact, the goddesses of Babylonia exercised but little independent power, and, both in the ritual of worship and in the myths and stories told about the gods, they play a very unimportant and subordinate part.

There is <u>one very striking exception</u> to this general rule, namely the <u>goddess Ishtar.</u> This deity in her own person appears to have absorbed the power and influence which were, at times, ascribed to other goddesses. She was identified with the Sumerian goddess Ninni, and in the Assyrian inscriptions she becomes the wife of the national god Ashur; she was also referred to as "Bēlit," *i.e.*, "the Lady," and in this character she assumed the titles and prerogatives of the wife of Bēl. In course of time the name "Ishtar" was employed as a generic term for goddess. In Babylonia, moreover, she was known by two different local names, which represented two quite distinct and separate characters. Under the title Anunitu she was worshipped as the goddess of battle at Agade and also at the city called Sippar of Anunitu; and under this aspect she was regarded as the daughter of Sin the Moon-god and of Ningal his wife. At the great temple of E-ana at Erech, on the other hand, she was worshipped as the goddess of love and identified with Nanā; and in this character she was regarded as the daughter of Anu and Anatu. It was in her gentler character as the goddess of love that she became connected in legend with Dumuzi or Tammuz, her lover who died in early youth, and for the sake of whose recovery she descended to the realm of the dead. She was served at Erech by numerous priestesses attached to her worship, and the rites practised at her shrine, a later form of which is described by Herodotus,[1] were performed in her honour as the goddess of love. By the Assyrians she was chiefly revered as the goddess of battle; she had two famous shrines in Assyria, one at Nineveh and one at Arbela, and at both she was worshipped in her warlike character.

Such are the characteristics of the principal gods of the Babylonians during the greater part of their history, and the sketch here given, though drawn from the religious and historical literature, is not inconsistent with the attributes assigned to them in the astrological and astronomical inscriptions. The identification of the planets with some of the greater gods was probably neither a very early nor primitive development, but one which took place after the Babylonian company of the gods had been definitely formed. When the worship of a host of local gods had given place to an organized system of nature worship, and when the growth of legend and myth necessitated a belief in the constant intercourse of the gods with one another, it was not unnatural for the Babylonians to assume that the gods dwelt together in some special place, that is to say in heaven. From the earliest times the sun and moon were regarded as the symbols of the gods Shamash and Sin respectively, and the movements of the two great luminaries were believed to be directed by them. At a later period the movements of the planets

---

[1] Book I., chap. 199.

were also thought to be directed by gods whose symbols they were, and it is probable that in this way the identification of Marduk with Jupiter, of Ishtar with Venus, of Ninib with Saturn, of Nergal with Mars and of Nabū with Mercury took place.[1] The members of the great triad of deities, who have been referred to as standing at the head of the company of the gods, were not omitted from this process; Bēl and Ea were transferred to heaven and placed side by side with Anu, and the three henceforth divided the heavens between them.

In the above sketch we have only enumerated the *ilāni rabūti*, or "great gods" of the Babylonians, and it must not be forgotten that subordinate to them stood a host of lesser gods as well as countless demons and spirits possessing various powers and influences. Of these lesser spirits the two classes most frequently met with in the religious inscriptions are the ANUNNAKI and the IGIGI, the "Spirits of the Earth" and the "Spirits of Heaven," respectively. Each class is generally mentioned in connection with the other, and they are described as carrying out the will of the great gods. In the magical literature the number of demons and ghosts and spirits which were hostile to mankind is very numerous, and to escape their evil influence it was necessary to invoke the assistance of magic and to employ powerful spells; by these means the help and protection of the great gods might be obtained to deliver a man from their baneful acts.

[1] See Jensen, *Die Kosmologie der Babylonier*, pp. 134 ff.

CHAPTER II.

HEAVEN, EARTH, AND HELL.

THE conception formed by the Babylonians with regard to the shape and nature of the earth on which they lived, and the ideas they held respecting the structure of the heavens, and the expectation which they entertained of one day dwelling in some region beyond the grave, can only be gathered from various stray references and allusions scattered throughout the remains of their literature. We possess no treatise on these subjects from the pen of a Babylonian priest, and we have to trace for ourselves and piece together the beliefs of the Babylonians on all these questions from passages in their historical and religious writings. That the ancient Babylonians concerned themselves with such problems there is ample evidence to show, and, although they have left behind them no detailed description of the universe, it is possible by a careful study of the texts to obtain a fairly complete idea of the world as they pictured it. To understand many of the legends and stories told concerning the Babylonian gods and heroes it is necessary to consider heaven, earth, and hell from their standpoint; it will be well, therefore, to trace their views concerning these regions before passing to the myths and legends that are translated or referred to in the following chapters.

With regard to the formation and shape of the earth we find a very interesting passage in a legend told concerning the old Babylonian hero Etana. The Eagle was a friend of Etana, and on one occasion this bird offered to carry him up to heaven. Etana accepted the Eagle's offer, and, clinging with his hands to the Eagle's pinions, he was carried up from the earth. As they rose together into the higher regions, the Eagle told Etana to look at the earth which grew smaller and smaller as they ascended; three times at different points of his flight, he told him to look down, and each time the Eagle spoke he compared the earth to some fresh object. After an interval of two hours the Eagle said, " Look, " my friend, at the appearance of the earth. Behold, " the sea, at its side is the House of Wisdom.[1] Look how " the earth resembles a mountain, the sea has turned into " [a pool of] water." After carrying Etana up for two more hours the Eagle said, " Look, my friend, at the " appearance of the earth. The sea is a girdle round the " earth." After ascending for a further space of two hours the Eagle exclaimed, " The sea has changed into a " gardener's channel"; and at a still higher point of their

---

[1] *I.e.*, the dwelling-place of Ea, the Lord of Wisdom, who dwelt in the deep.

flight the earth had shrunk to the size of a flower-bed. From these passages we see that the writer of the legend imagined the earth to be like a mountain around which flowed the sea. At the first stopping place Etana and the Eagle were so high that the sea looked like a pool of water, in the middle of which the earth rose. Later the sea had become so small that it looked like a girdle round the earth, and at length it appeared very little larger than a "gardener's water-channel" made for irrigation purposes.

The belief that the earth was hemispherical in shape, resembling a mountain with gently sloping sides, was common among the Babylonians as we know from other passages. According to Diodorus Siculus,[1] the Babylonians said that the earth was "like a boat and "hollow."[2] The boat used on the Tigris and Euphrates, and representations of which frequently occur on the monuments, had no keel and was circular in shape.[3] Such a boat turned upside down would give a very accurate picture of the Babylonian notion of the shape of the earth, the base of which the sea encircled as a

[1] A Greek historian, born in Sicily, who lived in the first century before Christ, and wrote a history of the world in forty books.
[2] Bk. II., ch. 31, ed. Vogel, vol. i., p. 222.
[3] The boats used by the Babylonians and Assyrians are also described by Herodotus (Bk. I., chap. 194), who says that they were circular like a shield, their ribs being formed by willow branches and covered externally with skins, while no distinction was made between the head and the stern. At the present day similar vessels built of branches and skins, over which bitumen is smeared, are used at Baghdad. (See Layard, *Nineveh and its Remains*, vol. ii. p. 381.)

girdle encircles a man. To a dweller on the plains of Mesopotamia the earth might well seem to be a mountain the centre of which was formed by the high mountain ranges of Kurdistan; while the Persian Gulf and the Indian Ocean which were on the south-east of Babylonia, and the Red Sea and the Mediterranean lying to the south-west and west respectively, doubtless led to the belief that the ocean surrounded the world.

At some distance above the earth was stretched out the heaven, a solid dome or covering in the form of a hollow hemisphere, very much like the earth in shape. Both earth and heaven rested upon a great body of water called Apsū, *i.e.*, the Deep. It is not quite certain how the solid dome of heaven was supported, that is to say, it is not clear whether it was supported by the earth, or was held up, independently of the earth, by the waters. According to one view the edge of the earth was turned up and formed around it a solid wall like a steep range of hills upon which the dome of heaven rested; and in the hollow between the mountain of the earth and this outer wall of hills the sea collected in the form of a narrow stream. This conception coincides with some of the phrases in the legend of Etana, but against it may be urged the fact that the sea is frequently identified with Apsū or the primeval Deep upon which the earth rested. But if the edges of the earth supported the dome of heaven, all communication between the sea and Apsū would be cut off. It is more probable therefore that the earth did not support the heaven, and that the foundations of the heavens, like those of the earth, rested on Apsū. In the beginning, before the creation of the world, nothing existed except the water wherein dwelt monsters. According to a version of the creation story, however, the god Bēl or Marduk formed the heavens and the earth out of the body of a great female monster that dwelt in the Deep which he had slain. Splitting her body into two halves, he fashioned from one half the dome of heaven, and from the other the earth.[1]

Above the dome of heaven was another mass of water, a heavenly ocean, which the solid dome of heaven supported and kept in its place, so that it might not break through and flood the earth. On the under side of the dome the stars had their courses and the Moon-god his path. In the dome, moreover, were two gates, one in the east and the other in the west, for the use of Shamash, the Sun-god, who every day journeyed from one to the other across the world. Coming from behind the dome of heaven, he passed through the eastern gate, and, stepping out upon the Mountain of the Sunrise at the edge of the world, he began his journey across the sky. In the evening he came to the Mountain of the Sunset, and, stepping upon it, he passed through the western gate of heaven

[1] See below, p. 55.

and disappeared from the sight of men. According to one tradition he made his daily journey across the sky in a chariot, which was drawn by two fiery horses. In representations on cylinder-seals, however, he is generally shown making his journey on foot. In the accompanying illustration Shamash is seen appearing

Shamash, the Sun-god, coming forth through the eastern door of heaven. (From a cylinder-seal in the British Museum, No. 89,110.)

above the horizon of the world, as he enters the sky through the eastern gate of heaven.

In the following hymn, addressed to the Rising Sun, a reference is made to Shamash entering the world through the eastern gate of heaven:—

"O Shamash, on the foundation of heaven thou hast flamed forth.
"Thou hast unbarred the bright heavens,
"Thou hast opened the portals of the sky.
"O Shamash, thou hast raised thy head over the land.
"O Shamash, thou hast covered the lands with the brightness of heaven."

Another hymn, addressed to the Setting Sun, contains a reference to the return of Shamash into the interior of heaven :—

"O Shamash, when thou enterest into the midst of heaven,
"The gate-bolt of the bright heavens shall give thee greeting,
"The doors of heaven shall bless thee.
"The righteousness of thy beloved servant shall direct thee.
"Thy sovereignty shall be glorious in E-babbara, the seat of thy power,
"And Ai, thy beloved wife, shall come joyfully into thy presence,
"And she shall give rest unto thy heart.
"A feast for thy godhead shall be spread for thee.
"O valiant hero, Shamash, [mankind] shall glorify thee.
"O lord of E-babbara, the course of thy path shall be straight.
"Go forward on the road which is a sure foundation for thee.
"O Shamash, thou art the judge of the world, thou directest the decisions thereof."

Each evening when Shamash entered the innermost part of heaven he was met by Ai, his wife, and he feasted and rested from his exertions in the abode of the gods. For, beyond the sky which was visible to men, and beyond the heavenly ocean which the dome of the sky supported, was a mysterious realm of transcendental splendour and beauty, the Kirib Shamē, or "Innermost part of Heaven," where the great gods at times dwelt apart from mankind. As a general rule the greater number of the gods dwelt upon earth, each in his own city and shrine, and each was believed to be intent upon the welfare of his worshippers; but at any moment they could, if they so desired, go up to heaven. Thus, the goddess Ishtar was wont to dwell in the ancient city of Erech, but when she thought that an insult had been offered to her divinity by the hero Gilgamesh she at once ascended into heaven and demanded vengeance from her father and mother, that is to say, Anu the god of heaven, and Anatu his wife.[1] Again, the deluge sent by Bēl upon the earth, besides destroying mankind, overwhelmed the shrines and temples of the gods who dwelt in the land, and they were driven forth and fled in fear to heaven, the realm of Anu.[2] It was, however, only upon rare occasions that the gods left the earth, and it is in accordance with this rule that the council-chamber of the gods, where fate and destiny were decreed, was not in heaven but upon the earth. The name of this chamber was Upshukkinaku, and here the gods gathered together when they were summoned to a general council. This chamber was supposed to

---

[1] See p. 161. [2] See p. 134.

be situated in the east, in the Mountain of the Sunrise, not far from the edge of the world where it was bounded by the waters of the great Deep.

It has already been stated that the earth was thought by the Babylonians to be in the form of a great hemisphere, and we must now add that they believed its hollow interior to be filled with the waters of the Deep upon which it also rested. The layer of earth was not, however, regarded as a thin crust. On the contrary, though hollow, the crust of solid ground was throught to be of great thickness. Within this crust, which formed the "mountain of the world," deep down below the surface of the ground, was a great cavern called ARALLŪ, and here was the abode of the dead. In this region was the great HOUSE OF THE DEAD which was surrounded by seven walls; these were so strongly built, and so carefully watched and guarded by beings of the underworld, that no one who had once entered therein could ever hope to return again to earth; indeed another name for Arallū, or the underworld, was *māt lā tāri*, "The land of no return." The House of the Dead was dark and gloomy, and in it the dead dragged out a weary and miserable existence. They never beheld the light of the sun, but sat in unchanging gloom. In appearance they resembled birds, for they were clothed in garments of feathers; their only food was dust and mud, and over everything thick dust was scattered. The Babylonians had no hope of a joyous life beyond the grave, and they did not conceive a paradise in which the deceased would live a life similar to that he lived upon earth. They made no distinction between the just and the unjust, and the good and the bad, but believed that all would share a common fate and would be reduced to the same level after death. The Babylonians shared this conception of the joyless condition of the dead with the Hebrews, by whom Sheōl, or Hell, was thought to be a place where the dead led an existence deprived of all the joys of life. In Isaiah the dead, including "the chief ones of the earth" and "the kings of the "nations," are pictured as trooping forth to meet the king of Babylon when he joins their company; and they answer and say unto him: "Art thou also become "weak as we? Art thou become like unto us? Thy "pomp is brought down to hell and the noise of thy "viols: the worm is spread under thee and worms "cover thee."[1] Ezekiel also emphasizes the same contrast between the condition of the living and the dead. Those that have caused terror in the land of the living, when they are slain lie still, and "bear their "shame with those that go down to the pit."[2] The Psalmist prays to Jehovah for deliverance, "for in "death there is no remembrance of thee: in Sheol who "shall give thee thanks?"[3]

The goddess who presided over this joyless realm

---

[1] Isaiah xiv. 10 f.   [2] Ezekiel xxxii. 17 ff.   [3] Psalm vi. 5.

of the dead was named ALLATU, or ERESHKIGAL, and she was associated in her rule with the god NERGAL in his character as the god of the dead. The name of the wife of Nergal was the goddess Laz, but legend tells how Nergal forced his way into the Lower World with the purpose of slaying Allatu, and how the goddess by her entreaties prevailed on him to spare her life and marry her. Henceforth Nergal and Allatu ruled together over the realm of the dead. The chief minister of Allatu was NAMTAR, the demon of pestilence and disease, who acted as her messenger and put her orders into execution. Allatu's decrees were written down by a goddess called BĒLIT-TSĒRI, "the "Lady of the Desert," who possibly took her name from the wild and barren desert that shut in Babylonia on the west; and the chief porter who guarded its entrance was a god named NEDU. The Anunnaki, or "Spirit of the Earth," also frequently acted under the orders of Nergal and Allatu. In addition to these chief deities Allatu exercised control over a number of demons, who, like Namtar, spread plague and disease among mankind, and so brought fresh subjects to the realm of their mistress.

The form and appearance of certain of the gods and demons of the underworld may be gathered from a number of engraved bronze plates which have come down to us; these, it has been suggested, were intended to be placed as votive tablets in the graves of the dead. The accompanying illustration has been taken from the finest known specimen of this class of object which was purchased in Syria some twenty years ago; it had evidently been brought there from some ancient Babylonian city. On the back of this tablet is cut in relief the figure of a mythical winged beast with a lion's head; it stands on its hind legs and raises its head above the edge of the plate, the top of which it grasps with its fore paws. On the front of the tablet, which is here reproduced, a funereal scene is represented. The beast looking over the top of the tablet is identified by some with the god Nergal, who was believed to preside over the funeral rites which are being performed for the deceased.

It will be observed that the scene is divided by means of thick lines into four registers. The first register contains the emblems of a number of the gods. Here we have a group of seven small circles or stars, and a crescent, and a winged solar disk, and a circle containing an eight-rayed star, and a cylindrical, horned head-dress, and other objects. It has been suggested that these emblems had astrological significance,[1] and if this be the case they may perhaps represent a particular grouping of the stars of the heavens and so indicate the date of the death of the man for whose benefit the tablet was made. The occurrence of such emblems, however, is frequent, both

---

[1] See Clermont-Ganneau, *Rev. Archéol., Nouv. Sér.*, vol. 37, p. 343.

Bronze plate on which are depicted the gods of the dead in attendance upon a deceased person and certain demons and dwellers in the underworld. (From *Revue Archéologique, Nouv. Sér.*, Vol. 37.)

on royal monuments (*e.g.*, the stele of Ashur-nātsir-pal, and the stele of Shalmaneser II., and the rock inscription at Bavian), and on inscribed cylinder seals; and on these two classes of objects the emblems do not appear to have any astrological significance. It therefore seems more correct to explain their position at the head of the tablet by assuming that they are placed there as amulets to secure for the dead man the favour of the deities whose emblems they were.

The next three registers into which the rest of the scene is divided have been supposed to represent different stages in the upper and lower world. It is preferable, however, to suppose that the three groups of figures in the three registers are parts of one scene, though they are placed, as is frequently the case in archaic sculptures, one above the other. The whole scene represents the deceased lying on his bier, attended by demons and beings from the underworld. In the second register we have seven mythical creatures with the bodies of men and the heads of beasts. They all are clothed in long tunics which reach to the feet, and they all face towards the right, and the right hand of each is raised. Each being has the head of a different beast. Beginning on the right it will be seen that the first one has the head of a serpent, the second that of a bird, the third that of a horse, the fourth that of a ram, the fifth that of a bear, the sixth that of a hound, and the seventh that of a lion. Certain other gods or demons occur in the third register. The first one on the right, who is in the form of a bearded man, has his right hand raised in the same manner as the seven beings in the second register, and next to him stand two lion-headed creatures, clasping hands. All these gods or demons appear to belong to the region of the dead, and they seem to be guarding the bier of the deceased, who is lying upon it with hands clasped and raised above him. On the left is the deceased in his grave-clothes; at his head and feet stand two attendants, with their right hands raised, and they appear to be performing some mystic ceremony over the corpse. The dress of these attendants is remarkable, for they wear garments made in the form of a fish. Behind the attendant at the head of the bier is a stand for burning incense.

The most interesting figures on the plate are those in the fourth register, for they represent two of the chief deities of the underworld. The female figure in the centre is the goddess Allatu, the queen of the dead. She has the head of a lioness and the body of a woman; in each hand she grasps a serpent, and a lion hangs from each breast. She kneels upon a horse in a boat and is sailing over the "Waters of Death," which adjoin Apsû, the primeval ocean that rolls beneath the earth. The hideous, winged demon behind her is Namtar, the demon of the plague, who waits upon her and is ever ready to do her bidding. It is not certain

OTHER GRAVE-TABLETS. 43

what the objects in front of Allatu are, but it is probable that they are intended to represent the offerings which were placed in the grave with the deceased. The purpose of the tablet seems to have been to secure the safe passage of the dead man into Arallû, or the underworld.

A somewhat similar bronze tablet, but less well preserved, is in the Imperial Ottoman Museum at Constantinople, and is said to have been found at Surghûl in Southern Babylonia.[1] On the back of this tablet, beneath the feet of the monster who looks over the top, a space of four lines has been left blank to receive an inscription which would either record the name and titles of the deceased, or contain an incantation which was to be recited for his benefit. On the back of a similar, though somewhat smaller tablet that was evidently intended to be used for the same purpose (although it only represented the goddess Allatu, while the bier and the Plague-demon Namtar and the other gods or demons found on the larger tablets were wanting), a longer inscription was found. This tablet was published by Lajard, but the text is so badly copied that it cannot be read with certainty.[2] A still smaller tablet of the same character is preserved in the British Museum.[3]

[1] See the plate published by Scheil, *Recueil de Travaux*, Vol. XX., p. 55.
[2] See Lajard, *Recherches sur le culte . . . de Vénus*, pl. XVII., No. 1.
[3] No. 86,262.

Perhaps in no matter do the Babylonians afford a more striking contrast to the Egyptians than in the treatment of the dead. In the moist, alluvial soil of Mesopotamia the dead body fell quickly into decay, and in the absence of ranges of hills such as those which run on each side of the Nile Valley, the making of rock-hewn tombs in which the bodies of the dead might be preserved was impossible. It is to this fact, probably, that we may trace the ideas of the gloomy existence which the Babylonians believed they would lead when they passed beyond the grave. It must not be imagined, however, that the Babylonians attached no importance to the rites of burial. On the contrary, the greatest misfortune that could befall a man was to be deprived of burial, for, in this case, it was thought that his shade could not reach Arallû, and that it would have to wander disconsolately about the earth, where, driven by the pangs of hunger, it would be obliged to eat and drink any offal or leavings which it might find in the street. It was in order to ensure such a fate to his foes that Ashur-bāni-pal, on his conquest of Susa, caused the graves of the kings who had been dead and buried many years to be disturbed and their bones to be dragged to Assyria; and the same object prompted the mutilation of corpses on the battlefield and the casting forth of the dead bodies to be devoured by birds and beasts of prey.

To leave a body unburied, however, was not unattended with danger to the living, for the shade of the dead man, during its wanderings over the earth, might bewitch any person it met and cause him grievous sickness. The wandering shade of a man was called "ekimmu," *i.e.*, spectre, and the sorcerer and the witch claimed to possess the power of casting a spell whereby an "ekimmu" might be made to harass a man. On the other hand an "ekimmu" would sometimes settle on a man of its own accord, in the hope that its victim would give it burial in order to free himself from its clutches. We have in the British Museum an interesting incantation which was intended to be recited by a man on whom an "ekimmu" had fastened itself,[1] and from this we learn that a man, who had fallen sick in consequence, might cry aloud in his pain, saying:—

"O Ea, O Shamash, O Marduk, deliver me,
"And through your mercy let me have relief.
"O Shamash, a horrible spectre for many days
"Hath fastened itself on my back, and will not loose its hold upon me.
"The whole day long he persecuteth me, and in the night season he striketh terror into me.
"He sendeth forth pollution, he maketh the hair of my head to stand up,
"He taketh the power from my body, he maketh mine eyes to start out,

[1] See King, *Babylonian Magic and Sorcery*, p. 119 f.

"He plagueth my back, he poisoneth my flesh,
"He plagueth my whole body."

The sick man in his despair prays to Shamash to be delivered from the ekimmu, whoever he may be, saying :—

"Whether it be the spectre of one of my own family and kindred,
"Or the spectre of one who was murdered,
"Or whether it be the spectre of any other man that haunteth me."

In order to ensure the departure of the spectre to the underworld he next makes the necessary offerings which will cause the spirit of the unburied man to depart, and says :—

"A garment to clothe him, and shoes for his feet,
"And a girdle for his loins, and a skin of water for him to drink,
"And . . .[1] as food for his journey have I given him.
"Let him depart into the West,
"To Nedu, the chief Porter of the Underworld, I consign him.
"Let Nedu, the chief Porter of the Underworld, guard him securely,
"And may bolt and bar stand firm (over him)."

It is clear, therefore, that in their own interest, as well as in that of the deceased, a man's friends and relations took good care that he was buried with all

---

[1] I cannot translate the signs in the text here.

MOURNING FOR THE DEAD.

due respect, and ensured his safe journey to the lower world by placing in the grave offerings of meat and drink to sustain him by the way; such offerings were perhaps also intended to alleviate his unhappy lot after his arrival in the gloomy abode of the underworld. Not many details have come down to us with regard to the ceremonies that were performed at the grave, but we know that after a man's death his house was filled with mourners, both male and female, whom his family hired in order that they might give public expression to the grief occasioned by his death. Among the Assyrian letter-tablets in the British Museum there is one [1] which refers to the death of the reigning king and to the regulations for mourning that were to be observed at the court. "The king," the letter says, "is dead, and the inhabitants of the city of Ashur "weep." The writer of the letter then goes on to describe the departure of the governor of the city with his wife from the palace, the offering up of a sacrifice, and the wearing of mourning raiment by the whole court; and it finally states that arrangements had been made with a director of music to come with his female musicians and sing dirges in the presence of the court. The mourning on the death of a private citizen would of course be carried out on a more modest scale.

After the mourning for the dead man had been performed, his body, duly prepared for burial, was

[1] British Museum, No. 81-2-4, 65.

carried forth to the grave. That the burial of the dead with accompanying rites and offerings was practised in Babylonia from a remote period is proved by a representation on a stele which was set up to record the victories of Eannadu, an ancient king of the city of Shirpurla, who reigned in all probability before B.C. 4000. On a portion of this stele is a representation of the burial of those of his warriors who had fallen in battle. The dead are laid in rows, with head to feet alternately, and above them a mound of earth has been raised; their comrades are represented bearing baskets containing more earth for the mound, or perhaps funeral offerings for the dead.[1] On the monuments of later Babylonian and Assyrian kings we do not find any representation of burial ceremonies, but in a broken inscription of one of the later Assyrian kings, whose name has unfortunately not been preserved, we have a brief but very interesting account of the ceremonies which he performed at his father's burial.[2] He says—

"Within the grave,
"The secret place,
"In kingly oil,
"I gently laid him.
"The grave-stone
"Marketh his resting-place.
"With mighty bronze

---

[1] See De Sarzec, *Découvertes en Chaldée*, pl. 3.
[2] British Museum, K. 7856; see Meissner, *Vienna Oriental Journal*, Vol. XII., pp. 60 ff.

THE INTERMENT OF A KING. 49

"I sealed its entrance,
"I protected it with an incantation.
"Vessels of gold and silver,
"Such as (my father) loved,
"All the furniture that befitteth the grave,
"The due right of his sovereignty,
"I displayed before the Sun-god,
"And beside the father who begat me,
"I set them in the grave.
"Gifts unto the princes,
"Unto the Spirits of the Earth,[1]
"And unto the gods who inhabit the grave,
"I then presented."

From this we learn that the king placed vessels of gold and silver in the grave as dedicatory offerings, and after sealing up the entrance to the grave he pronounced a powerful spell to prevent the violation of the tomb by robbers; he also presented offerings to propitiate the demons and dwellers in the underworld.

Another interesting point about this record is the fact that the dead body is said to have been set "in "kingly oil," for the oil was clearly used with the idea of preserving the body from decay. Salt also seems to have been used for the purpose of preserving the dead, for Ashur-bāni-pal tells how, when Nabū-bēl-shumāti had caused himself to be slain by his attendant to prevent himself falling alive into the

[1] The Anunnaki.

BAB. REL. E

hands of Ashur-bāni-pal, Ummanaldas had the body placed in salt and conveyed to Assyria into the presence of the king.[1] Besides salt and oil, honey seems also to have been used by the Babylonians for preserving the dead. Herodotus says that the Babylonians buried in honey,[2] and that honey possesses great powers of preserving the dead is proved by the fact that the Egyptians also used it for this purpose.[3] Moreover, it is recorded that Alexander the Great when on his death-bed commanded that he should be buried in honey, and it seems that his orders were obeyed.[4] Tradition also says that one Marcellus having prepared the body of Saint Peter for burial by means of large quantities of myrrh, spices, etc., laid it in a "long chest" filled with honey.[5]

There is ample evidence, therefore, to show that the Babylonians cared for their dead and took pains about their burial, and it is the more surprising on that account, that during the numerous excavations which have been carried out in Mesopotamia, comparatively few graves have been discovered. Of the graves that have been found, some are built of bricks and are in the form of small vaulted chambers, while others have a flat or domed roof supported by a brick substructure;

---

[1] *Cuneiform Inscriptions of Western Asia*, Vol. V., pl. vii., ll. 38 ff.
[2] Bk. I., chap. 198.   [3] See Budge, *The Mummy*, p. 183.
[4] See Budge, *The Life and Exploits of Alexander the Great*, Vol. II., p. 349 f.
[5] See Brit. Mus. MS. Oriental 678, fol. 17a, col. 1.

in addition to these graves a few clay sarcophagi and burial jars have been found. With the skeletons in the graves are usually found a small number of vases and perhaps some simple objects of the toilet; but from the fact that no inscriptions have been found either over these graves or upon any of the objects found therein, it is extremely difficult to assign to them even an approximate date; in fact, some have unhesitatingly assigned them to a period which is much later than that of the ancient Babylonian and Assyrian empires. To account for this dearth of graves the suggestion has been made that the Babylonians burnt their dead, but not a single passage has been found in the cuneiform inscriptions in support of this view. It is true that in the winter of 1886 and in the spring of the following year the Royal Prussian Museum sent out an expedition to Babylonia, which, after excavating the mounds of Surghūl and El-Hibbah, thought they had obtained conclusive evidence that the Babylonians burnt their dead.[1] But it has since been pointed out that the tombs they excavated belong to a period subsequent to the fall of the Babylonian Empire, while the half-burned appearance of the charred human remains they discovered seemed to suggest that the bodies were not cremated but were accidentally destroyed by fire. However the comparatively small number of graves that have been found may be

[1] See Koldewey, *Zeitschrift für Assyriologie*, Bd. II., pp. 403 ff.

accounted for, we may confidently believe that the Babylonians and Assyrians were in the habit of burying, and not burning, their dead throughout the whole course of their history. We are right also in saying that they imagined that burial, and offerings made at the tomb, would ameliorate the lot of the departed, and that they were usually scrupulous in performing all rites which could possibly benefit the dead.

CHAPTER III.

THE LEGENDS OF CREATION.

THE nations of the ancient world who have left behind any remains or traces of their literature possessed theories as to the manner in which the world came into being. Such theories, or cosmogonies as they are termed, are generally told in the form of myths or stories, and, although we only know them in their later and fully developed forms, their origin may be assumed to go back to a considerable antiquity. If we may judge from the studies and observations that have been made of undeveloped races at the present day, it may be concluded that primitive man was essentially a maker of myths. Believing as he did that every object and force in nature possessed a personality and will like his own, he would explain the changes he saw taking place in the world around him by means of legends and stories. In these he would ascribe to the mysterious beings, which seemed to him to animate the natural world, motives similar to those which would control his own actions. At a more mature stage in his development he began to perceive a connection or dependence between the various powers of nature, such as the alternation of day and night, the movements of the stars, and the regular recurrence of the seasons; these would tend to suggest that some plan or system had been followed in the creation of the world, and in seeking for the reason of things along the familiar lines of myth, he would in process of time develop a cosmogony or story of creation. We have evidence that at least two such stories were current in Babylonia and Assyria in the later periods of their history.

The story of the creation of the world as told in Babylon about the year B.C. 300 we know in brief outline from the extracts that have come down to us from the history of Berosus, a Chaldean priest, who ministered in the temple of Bēl at Babylon at the end of the fourth and the beginning of the third century before Christ. Berosus wrote a history of Babylonia, beginning with the creation of the world and extending down to his own time, and although his work, which he translated into Greek, has been lost, extracts from it have been preserved in the books of later writers. His account of the creation, for instance, was reproduced by Alexander Polyhistor, from whom Eusebius quotes in the first book of his *Chronicon*.[1] From this we learn that the Babylonians pictured to themselves

---

[1] *Chron.* I., ed. Schoene, col. 14 ff.

THE VERSION OF BEROSUS. 55

a time when the world had no existence, a time before things came into being, when darkness and water alone existed. The water, however, did not remain uninhabited for long, for monsters arose in it, *i.e.*, men with wings, and creatures with four wings and two human heads, and beings with two heads, one male and one female. Some creatures had the bodies of men, but had the feet and horns of goats; some had the legs of horses, and others, like hippocentaurs, had the bodies and legs of horses but the upper parts of a man. Others, again, were in the form of bulls with the heads of men, or dogs with four bodies ending in the tail of a fish, or men and horses with the heads of dogs, and some had the head and body of a horse but the tail of a fish. In the water also creeping things, and serpents, and many other monsters of strange and varied shapes existed. Over these monsters a woman reigned called Omoroka (or Omorka), in Chaldee Thamte,[1] or in Greek Thalassa, "the Sea." A change in this world of chaos was brought about by the death of the woman Omorka, who was slain by a god named Bēl. Bēl cleft her in twain, and from one half he made the earth, and from the other he made the heavens; and he slew also the monsters of the deep over whom she ruled. The account then goes on to say that after Bēl had created the earth, he perceived that it was barren

---

[1] The text reads *Thalatth*, which is probably a corruption of *Thamte*, *i.e.*, *tāmtu* the Babylonian for "sea, ocean." See Robertson Smith, *Zeitschrift für Assyriologie*, Bd VI., p. 339.

and had no inhabitants; he therefore decided to use his own blood for creation. He bade one of the gods to cut off his head and mix the earth with the blood which flowed from him, and from the mixture he directed him to fashion men and animals. Although deprived of his head Bēl did not die, for he is said to have also created the stars, the sun and moon, and the five planets, after his head was cut off. Such is the account of the Babylonian cosmogony as narrated by Berosus, which Eusebius has preserved. But as the latter writer quoted the story at second hand, it is more than probable that he accidentally misrepresented or misunderstood certain portions of it.

Fortunately we have not to depend on Eusebius alone for our knowledge of the Babylonian stories of creation, for we now possess far fuller accounts on Assyrian and Babylonian tablets which have been published within the last twenty-five years. The credit of having made known to the world the Babylonian Creation tablets belongs to the late Mr. George Smith who, in 1875, published a story very like that told by Berosus, inscribed upon some of the tablets and fragments of tablets that had been brought to England from the site of Ashur-bāni-pal's library at Nineveh several years before. The publication of the text and translations of the Creation tablets by Mr. Smith[1] threw

---

[1] See *Trans. Soc. Bibl. Arch.*, Vol. IV. (1876) p. 363 f. (six plates), and *The Chaldean Account of Genesis*, London, 1876.

great light upon the Babylonian cosmogony, and evoked considerable interest in the subject.

From the date of their first publication the tablets have been closely studied, and from time to time fresh fragments of the legend have been identified in the British Museum. During this period, moreover, the knowledge of the Assyrian language has greatly increased, so that a more accurate rendering of the texts can now be given than was possible at the time of their discovery.[1] From these inscriptions we gather that at about the middle of the seventh century before Christ the Babylonian story of the creation was preserved at Nineveh, the capital of Assyria, in the form of a great poem, divided into a number of parts or sections, each of which was inscribed upon a separate tablet. The tablets were distinguished by numbers, and the whole series was named ENUMA ELISH, "When in the height," from the opening words of the First Tablet. The poem is incomplete in passages, and the end is very imperfect. We know that the series when complete contained at least six tablets, but it is impossible to say definitely how many tablets it originally contained. In spite of the fragmentary condition of many parts of the poem, however, the thread of the narrative can generally be followed.

[1] For the principal works dealing with the Creation tablets which have been published within recent years, see Jensen, *Die Kosmologie der Babylonier*, pp. 263 ff., Gunkel and Zimmern, *Schöpfung und Chaos*, pp. 401 ff., and Delitzsch, *Das babylonische Weltschöpfungsepos*, pp. 7 ff.

58 SUMMARY OF THE BABYLONIAN LEGEND.

This version of the Babylonian cosmogony is practically identical with that given by Berosus about three hundred and fifty years later. According to the version on the Assyrian tablets, chaos in the beginning, before the world was created, consisted of a watery mass. Two primeval beings personified chaos, namely APSŪ, the "Deep," and TIĀMAT, the universal mother, who corresponds to the woman named Omorka, or Thamte, by Berosus. Beside Apsū and Tiāmat no other being existed, and they mingled their waters in confusion. In the course of time the gods were created; the first were Lakhmu and Lakhamu, Anshar and Kishar came next, after many ages, and after a further period the other great gods were born. But Tiāmat, the monster of the Deep, who had taken the form of a huge serpent, and Apsū, her consort, revolted against the gods, and created a brood of monsters to destroy them. Anshar, the leader of the gods, having entrusted in vain the god Anu, and after him the god Ea, with the task of resisting Tiāmat, prevailed on Marduk, the son of Ea, to be the champion of the gods and to do battle with the monster. The gods were summoned by Anshar to a council that they might confer supreme power upon Marduk and arm him for the fight. After completing his preparations Marduk went out to meet Tiāmat and her host and succeeded in slaying her and in taking her helpers captive. He then split Tiāmat's body in half and from one half he formed the heaven, fixing it as a firmament to divide the upper from the lower waters, and placing bars and sentinels that the waters should not break through. Marduk then created the heavenly bodies that they might regulate the seasons, and he appointed the moon to rule the night. The poem at this point becomes mutilated, but there is evidence to show that Marduk then created the earth, and the green herb, and cattle, and the beasts of the field, and creeping things, and man, in the order here given.

From the above summary of the Babylonian story of creation it will be seen that it presents some very remarkable points of resemblance to the narrative of the creation as preserved in the first chapter of Genesis; and it is chiefly to this fact that the widespread interest in the legend is due. The bare outline given by Berosus does not suggest a very close parallel to the Biblical account, but from the more detailed narrative as given on the tablets we see that many features of the story of creation narrated in Genesis are also characteristic of the Babylonian cosmogony. Thus according to each account the existence of a watery chaos preceded the creation of the present world. The Hebrew word *tehōm* translated "the deep" in Genesis,[1] corresponds exactly with the Babylonian "Tiāmat," the monster of the deep who personified chaos and confusion. The creation of light recorded in Genesis is the equivalent of the statement on the Creation tablets

[1] Gen. i. 2.

that Tiāmat was vanquished by Marduk, for he overcame the monster in his character as a solar god. Then there follows in each narrative the description of the creation of a firmament, or solid dome of heaven, to keep the upper waters in place; in each account the narrative of the creation of the heavenly bodies follows that of the firmament, and in each also they are appointed to regulate the seasons. It has been suggested that the seven days of creation in Genesis correspond to seven definite acts of creation in the Babylonian account; but a careful study of the Babylonian poem has shown that such an arrangement was not contemplated by the Babylonian scribes, nor is there any evidence to show that the creation was deliberately classified in a series of seven acts. A slight perusal of the legend is, however, sufficient to prove that the two accounts present in many ways a very striking resemblance to each other; but in some respects the contrast they present is no less striking. When we examine the aims and ideas which underlie and permeate the two narratives, all resemblance between them ceases. The monotheism of Genesis finds no echo in the Babylonian poem, and in the latter no single and pre-existing deity created the universe from chaos by his word, but the gods themselves emerged from chaos, and it was only after one of their number had fought with and slain the mother of them all that the creation of the world took place.

THE CREATION OF THE GODS. 61

Before we proceed to consider the problem of the relationship of these two stories of the creation it will be well to give a translation of those portions of the Babylonian legends that have been preserved, and to trace their age and history so far as they can be ascertained.

The beginning of the First Tablet contains a description of chaos and of the birth of the oldest gods; it reads:—

"When in the height heaven was not named,
"And the earth beneath did not yet bear a name; [1]
"And Apsū the primeval, who begat them,
"And chaos, Tiāmat, the mother of them both—
"Their waters were mingled together, and
"No field was formed, no marsh was to be seen;
"When of the gods none had been called into being,
"And none bore a name, and no destinies [were ordained];
"Then were created the gods, [all of them],
"Lakhmu and Lakhamu were called into being. . .
"Ages increased . . . .
"Anshar and Kishar were created . . . . . .
"Long were the days . . . .
"Anu, the father . . . .
"Anshar and Anu . . . ."

The last line but one evidently refers to the creation

---

[1] According to Semitic ideas the name of a thing was regarded as its essence; hence to bear a name was equivalent to being in existence.

of the god Anu; and from a passage in Damascius, where this Babylonian theogony is reproduced,[1] we may infer that the gods Bēl and Ea were created along with him. It is probable that the creation of the other great gods was then described. Chaos was, in fact, giving place to order, but the gods were not for long allowed to remain in peace, for Tiāmat, their mother, conceived a hatred for them, and with Apsū, their father, plotted their destruction. The First Tablet ends with a description of the brood of monsters which Tiāmat spawned to aid her in her fight with the gods.

Of the Second Tablet very little has been preserved, but, as in the case of the First Tablet, sufficient fragments of the text remain to indicate the general course of the story. The piecing together of the narrative, however, would be well nigh impossible were it not for a strange characteristic of Babylonian poetry, that is to say, the practice of frequent repetition. But for this practice the description of Tiāmat's brood of monsters, and of her selection of Kingu as their captain would be lost, for hardly any of it remains on the fragments of the First Tablet. The description, however, is repeated in the form of a message to the god Anshar at the beginning of the Second Tablet; it is also repeated on the Third Tablet, once by Anshar to his minister Gaga, and again by Gaga when delivering Anshar's message to Lakhmu and Lakhamu. Had we

---

[1] *Quaestiones de primis principiis*, chap. 125 (ed. Kopp, p. 384).

ANSHAR'S INSTRUCTIONS TO GAGA. 63

the complete text of the First and Second Tablets of the poem such repetition might be wearisome, but in their present imperfect condition its advantages for the restoration of the text are obvious.

On hearing the news of Tiāmat's preparations for battle the god Anshar was troubled, and he sent his son Anu to speak with her and to try to appease her anger. Anu went to her, but when he saw her he turned back in fear. The god Ea was next sent by Anshar, but he met with no better success. Anshar then invited the god Marduk to do battle with Tiāmat, and he consented on condition that the gods would meet together and solemnly declare him their champion. The Second Tablet ends with Marduk's speech to Anshar, and the Third Tablet opens with Anshar's instructions to his minister Gaga to summon a council of the gods. Gaga was ordered to carry tidings of Tiāmat's revolt to Lakhmu and Lakhamu, and to direct them to summon the gods who were to appoint Marduk as their champion. The Third Tablet begins:—

"Anshar opened his mouth, and

"[To Gaga] his minister spake the word:

"'[Go Gaga, thou minister] that rejoicest my spirit,

"[To Lakhmu and La]khamu I will send thee.

". . . . .

". . . . . let the gods, all of them,

"[Make ready for a feast], at a banquet let them sit,

"[Let them eat bread], let them mix wine,
"[That for Marduk], their [avenger], they may decree the fate.
"[Go Ga]ga, stand before them,
"[And all that I] tell thee, repeat unto them, (and say):
"'Anshar your son has sent me,
"The purpose of his heart he has made known to me.
"He says that Tiāmat our mother has conceived a hatred for us,
"With all her force she rages, full of wrath.
"All the gods have turned to her;
"With those, whom you created, they go at her side.
"They are banded together, and at the side of Tiāmat they advance;
"They are furious, they devise mischief without resting night and day.
"They prepare for battle, fuming and raging;
"They have joined their forces and are making war.
"Ummu-Khubur,[1] who formed all things,
"Has made in addition weapons invincible, she has spawned monster-serpents,
"Sharp of tooth, and cruel of fang;
"With poison instead of blood she has filled their bodies.
"Fierce monster-vipers she has clothed with terror,

---

[1] Another name of Tiāmat.

"With splendour she has decked them, and she has caused them to [mount ?] on high.
"Whoever beholds them is overcome by dread.
"Their bodies rear up and none can withstand their attack.
"She has set up the viper, and the dragon, and the (monster) Lakhamu,
"And the hurricane, and the raging hound, and the scorpion-man,
"And mighty tempests, and the fish-man, and the ram;
"They bear merciless weapons, without fear of the fight.
"Her commands are mighty, none can resist them;
"After this fashion, huge of stature, she has made eleven (monsters).
"Among the gods who are her sons, inasmuch as he gave her support,
"She has exalted Kingu; in their midst she has raised him to power.
"To march before the forces, to lead the host,
"To give the battle-signal, to advance to the attack,
"To direct the battle, to control the fight,
"To him has she entrusted; in costly raiment she has made him sit, (saying):
"'I have uttered thy spell, in the assembly of the gods I have raised thee to power,
"The dominion over all the gods have I entrusted to thee.

"Be thou exalted, thou my chosen spouse,
"Let them magnify thy name over all [the world].'
"Then did she give him the Tablets of Destiny,[1] on his breast she laid them, (saying):
"'Thy command shall not be without avail, and the word of thy mouth shall be established.'
"Now Kingu, (thus) exalted, having received the power of Anu,
"Decreed the fate for the gods, her sons:
"'Let the opening of your mouth quench the Fire-god;
"Whoso prides himself on valour, let him display (his) might!'"

So far Anshar has described the revolt of Tiāmat and the creation of the monsters who were to help her in the fight, and her selection of Kingu as the captain of her host; all these things are described in the First Tablet in exactly the same language. He next mentions the measures he has taken on hearing of Tiāmat's treachery in the following words:—

"I sent Anu, but he was unable to go against her;
"Nudimmud[2] was afraid and turned back.
"Marduk has set out, the director of the gods, your son;

---

[1] The possession of the "Tablets of Destiny" carried with it supremacy among the gods; with a view of obtaining this supremacy the god Zū stole them from Bēl, but Shamash the Sun-god compelled him to restore them. See pp. 193 f.

[2] A title of the god Ea.

"To set out against Tiāmat his heart has prompted (him).
"He opened his mouth and spake unto me:
"'If I, your avenger,
"Conquer Tiāmat and give you life,
"Appoint an assembly, make my fate pre-eminent and proclaim it.
"In Upshukkinnaku[1] seat yourselves joyfully together.
"With my mouth like you will I decree fate.
"Whatsoever I do, shall remain unaltered,
"The word of my lips shall never be changed nor made of no avail.'
"Hasten therefore and swiftly decree for him the fate which you bestow,
"That he may go and fight your strong enemy!"
The narrative continues:—
"Gaga went, he took his way and
"Humbly before Lakhmu and Lakhamu, the gods, his fathers,
"He made obeisance, and he kissed the ground at their feet.
"He humbled himself; then he stood up and spake unto them."
Gaga then repeats the message which Anshar has given to him, but, as it corresponds word for word with the speech of Anshar quoted above, it may here

[1] The name of the place where the gods met together.

be omitted. The narrative describes the effect of Gaga's message in the following words :—

"Lakhmu and Lakhamu heard and [were afraid],
"All of the Igigi wailed bitterly, (saying):
"'What has been changed that they should conceive [this hatred]?
"We do not understand the deed of Tiāmat!'
"Then did they collect and go,
"The great gods, all of them, who decree fate.
"They entered in before Anshar, they filled [the chamber];
"They pressed on one another, in the assembly . . .
"They made ready for the feast, at the banquet they sat;
"They ate bread, they mixed sesame-wine.
"The sweet drink, the mead, confused their [senses],
"They became drunk with drinking, their bodies were filled (with meat and drink).
"Their limbs were wholly relaxed, and their spirit was exalted;
"Then for Marduk, their avenger, did they decree the fate."

At this point the Third Tablet of the series ends.

The Fourth Tablet opens with a description of the ceremony of decreeing fate for Marduk thus:—

"They prepared for him a lordly chamber,
"Before his fathers as counsellor he took his place."

When Marduk had taken his seat, the gods addressed him in the following words :—

"Thou art chiefest among the great gods,
"Thy fate is unequalled, thy word is Anu![1]
"O Marduk, thou art chiefest among the great gods,
"Thy fate is unequalled, thy word is Anu!
"Henceforth not without avail shall be thy command,
"In thy power shall it be to exalt and to abase.
"Established shall be the word of thy mouth, irresistible shall be thy command;
"None among the gods shall transgress thy boundary.
"Abundance, the desire of the shrines of the gods,
"Shall be established in thy sanctuary, even though they lack (offerings).
"O Marduk, thou art our avenger!
"We give thee sovereignty over the whole world.
"Sit thou down in majesty, be exalted in thy command.
"Thy weapon shall never lose its power, it shall crush thy foe.
"O lord, spare the life of him that putteth his trust in thee,
"But as for the god who led the rebellion,[2] pour out his life!"

---

[1] *I.e.*, "Thy word has the same power as that of Anu."
[2] Literally, "began the evil."

But before Marduk set out to do battle with Tiāmat, the gods wished him to put to the test the power which they had conferred upon him, and with this object in view they brought a garment into their midst, and then addressed their avenger, saying:—

"'May thy fate, O lord, be supreme among the gods,
"To destroy and to create; speak thou the word, and (thy command) shall be fulfilled.
"Command now and let the garment vanish;
"And speak the word again and let the garment reappear!'"

In obedience to the words of the gods Marduk

"Spake with his mouth, and the garment vanished;
"Again he commanded it, and the garment reappeared.
"When the gods, his fathers, beheld (the fulfilment of) his word,
"They rejoiced, and they did homage (unto him, saying), 'Marduk is king!'
"They bestowed upon him the sceptre, and the throne, and the ring,
"They gave him an invincible weapon, wherewith to overwhelm the foe.
"'Go,' (they said), 'and cut off the life of Tiāmat,
"And let the wind carry her blood into secret places.'
"(Thus) did the gods, his fathers, decree for the lord his fate;

"They caused him to set out on a path of prosperity and success.
"He made ready the bow, he girded his weapon upon him,
"He slung a spear upon him and fastened it, . . .
"He raised the club, in his right hand he grasped (it),
"The bow and the quiver he hung at his side.
"He set the lightning in front of him,
"With burning flame he filled his body.
"He made a net to enclose the inward parts of Tiāmat,
"The four winds he set so that nothing of her might escape;
"The South wind, and the North wind, and the East wind, and the West wind
"He brought near to the net which his father Anu had given him.
"He created the evil wind, and the storm, and the hurricane,
"The four-fold wind, and the seven fold wind, and the whirlwind, the wind which was without equal;
"He sent forth the winds which he had created, seven in all,
"To destroy the inward parts of Tiāmat; and they followed after him.
"Then the lord raised the thunderbolt, his mighty weapon,

"He mounted the chariot, an object unequalled for terror,

"He harnessed four horses and yoked them to it,

"[All of them] ferocious, and high of courage, and swift of pace;

"[They gnashed with] their teeth, their bodies were flecked with foam,

"They had been [trained to gallop], they had been taught to trample underfoot."

Thus, standing in his chariot, and followed by the seven winds he had created, did Marduk set out for the fight. His advance against Tiāmat in the sight of all the gods is described in the following words :—

"Then the lord drew nigh, on Tiāmat he gazed,

"He beheld the scorn (?) of Kingu, her spouse.

"As (Marduk) gazed, (Kingu) was troubled in his gait,

"His will was destroyed and his movements ceased.

"And the gods, his helpers, who marched by his side,

"Beheld their leader's [distress], and their sight was troubled."

But Tiāmat stood firm, with unbent neck, and taunted Marduk and the gods who were gathered in safety behind him; to these taunts Marduk replied by reproaching her with her treachery, and he bade her prepare for battle in these words:—

"'Let thy hosts be equipped, and let thy weapons be set in order!

THE DEATH OF TIĀMAT.

" Stand! I and thou, let us join battle!'
" When Tiāmat heard these words,
" She was like one possessed, she lost her senses,
" She uttered loud, angry cries.
" She trembled and shook to her very foundations.
" She recited an incantation, she pronounced her spell,
" And the gods of the battle cried out for their weapons.
" Then advanced Tiāmat and Marduk, the counsellor of the gods;
" To the fight they came on, to the battle they drew nigh.
" The lord spread out his net to catch her,
" The evil wind that was behind (him) he let loose in her face.
" As Tiāmat opened her mouth to its full extent,
" He drove in the evil wind, while as yet she had not shut her lips.
" The terrible winds filled her belly,
" And her courage was taken from her, and her mouth she opened wide.
" He seized the spear and broke through her belly,
" He severed her inward parts, he pierced her heart.
" He overcame her and cut off her life;
" He cast down her body and stood upon it.
" When he had slain Tiāmat, the leader,
" Her might was broken, her force was scattered,

"And the gods, her helpers, who marched by her side,
"Trembled, and were afraid, and turned back.
"They took to flight to save their lives;
"In an enclosure they were caught, they were not able to escape.
"He took them captive, he broke their weapons;
"In the net they were caught and in the snare they sat down.
"[The whole] world they filled with cries of grief.
"They received punishment from him, they were held in bondage.
"And on the eleven creatures whom she had filled with the power of striking terror,
"The troop of devils which marched at her bidding (?),
"He brought affliction, [he destroyed] their power;
"Them and their opposition he trampled under his feet.
"Moreover Kingu, who had been made leader [over all of] them,
"He conquered and like unto the god . . . he counted him.
"He took from Kingu the Tablets of Destiny that were not [rightly] his,
"He sealed them with a seal and on his own breast he laid them.
"Now after the valiant Marduk had conquered and destroyed his enemies,

The Fight between Marduk and Tiāmat. (From two limestone slabs in the British Museum, Nos. 28 and 29.)

"And had made the arrogant foe even like a broken reed (?),
"He fully established Anshar's triumph over the enemy,
"And attained the purpose of Nudimmud.
"Over the gods that were captive he strengthened his durance.
"To Tiāmat, whom he had conquered, he returned,
"And the lord stood upon Tiāmat's hinder parts;
"With his merciless club he smashed her skull;
"He cut the channels of her blood,
"He made the North wind bear it away into secret places.
"His fathers beheld, they rejoiced and were glad;
"Presents and gifts they brought unto him.
"Then the lord rested, and gazed on her dead body.
"He divided the flesh of the body, having devised a cunning plan.
"He split her up like a flat fish into two halves.
"One half of her he set in place as a covering for the heavens.
"He fixed a bolt, he stationed watchmen,
"And bade them not to let her waters come forth.
"He passed through the heavens, he surveyed the regions (thereof),
"Over against the Deep he set the dwelling of Nudimmud.
"And the lord measured the structure of the Deep,

"And he founded E-shara, a mansion like unto it.
"The mansion E-shara, which he created as heaven,
"He caused Anu, Bêl and Ea in their districts to inhabit."

With these words the Fourth Tablet of the series ends.

Marduk having conquered Tiâmat, thus began the work of creation. From one half of the monster's body he fashioned heaven in the form of a solid covering, which he also furnished with bolts and watchmen to keep the waters which were above it in their place. The dwelling of Nudimmud he fixed in the deep, *i.e.*, the abyss of waters beneath the earth, and he also founded E-shara. Some think that E-shara is the earth;[1] and according to this view Marduk may be regarded as having now created and set in place, the heavens, and the earth, and the waters which were beneath the earth. Others, however, consider E-shara to be a name for heaven, or for a part of it, and the last two lines of the Fourth Tablet of the poem certainly favour this view. The most natural meaning of the passage is that Marduk made the mansion of E-shara to be heaven, which he then divided between the three gods Anu, Bêl and Ea. Moreover we know from other sources that these three gods, in addition to ruling the heaven, and the earth, and the abyss respectively, in their astrological characters divided the heaven between

---

[1] See Jensen, *Die Kosmologie der Babylonier*, pp. 195 ff.

CREATION OF THE HEAVENLY BODIES. 79

them;[1] and the position of certain stars is noted in astrological tablets by apportioning them to the various dominions of these deities. According to the former view this passage in the poem means that Marduk created E-shara (the earth) "like a heavenly vault,"[2] *i.e.*, in the form of a hollow hemisphere like the firmament overhead; but to obtain this sense the ordinary meaning of the words has to be strained considerably.

In the Fifth Tablet of the series Marduk continued the work of creation. He had already portioned out the heavens and the abyss, and he now assigned to each part its separate function, and laid down laws for the regulation of the whole. The tablet describes the creation of the heavenly bodies and the regulation of the seasons, but unfortunately only the beginning part has been preserved. The text reads:—

"He made the stations for the great gods,
"The stars, their images, (and) the constellations he fixed;
"He ordained the year and into sections he divided it.
"For the twelve months he fixed three stars.
"From the day when the year comes forth[3] until (its) close,
"He founded the station of Nibir[4] to determine their bounds;

---

[1] See above, p. 26.
[2] See Jensen, *op. cit.*, p. 289.   [3] *I.e.*, begins.   [4] *I.e.*, Jupiter.

" That none might err or go astray,
" He set the stations of Bēl and Ea along with him.
" He opened great gates on both sides (of the firmament),
" He made strong the bolt on the left and on the right,
" In the midst thereof he fixed the zenith.
" The Moon-god he caused to shine forth, the night he entrusted to him.
" He appointed him, a being of the night, to determine the days.
" Every month without ceasing with the crown he covered (?) him, (saying):
" ' At the beginning of the month, at the shining of the . . . ,
" Thou shalt command the horns to determine six days,
" And on the seventh day to [divide] the crown.' "

Here the text becomes too broken to make a connected translation, though from what remains it may be gathered that Marduk continued to address the Moon-god, and to define his position with regard to Shamash, the Sun-god, at the different points of his course. What the actually missing portion of the text contained we cannot say with certainty, but we may conjecture that it described further acts of creation. That there was a Sixth Tablet is proved by the catch-line at the end of the Fifth Tablet, and the text of this also must have referred to the same subject. There is no evidence to show how many tablets were comprised in the Creation Series, although some have thought that the number was greater than six. Fragments of tablets have been found which refer to acts of creation, and as these cannot be fitted into places in the tablets already described, it has been suggested they formed parts of the tablets which seem to be missing. One such fragment is of especial interest, for it contains a reference to the creation of the " beasts of " the field, the cattle of the field, and the creeping " things of the field." It is improbable that the fragment belonged to the Creation Series, inasmuch as the gods as a body, and not Marduk alone, are credited by it with the creation of the world, and besides this the god Ea, Marduk's father, is mentioned as taking a prominent part in the work. The fragment in fact reproduces a variant form of the creation legend, but its description of the creation of the beasts may well be cited in favour of the view that some missing portion of the poem contained a similar episode. The fragment which contains the opening lines of the tablet begins :—

" When all the gods had made [the world],
" Had created the heavens, had formed [the earth],
" Had brought living creatures into being . . . ,
" The cattle of the field, the [beasts] of the field, and the creeping things [of the field], . . ."

The rest of the fragment is too broken to admit of a trustworthy restoration of the text, though the reference to Nin-igi-azag, *i.e.*, "the lord of clear vision," a title of the god Ea, seems to connect him with some further act of creation.

There are also some grounds for believing that in addition to the creation of animals some portion of the poem described the creation of mankind. A hymn has been found inscribed upon a tablet which contains a number of remarkable addresses in honour of the god Marduk, and, as many of them refer to his acts of creation, it has been thought that the composition formed the concluding tablet of the series.[1] After addressing him as one who shewed mercy to the gods he had taken captive, and who removed the yoke from the neck of the gods his enemies,[2] the hymn refers to his having created men and declares that his word shall be established and shall not be forgotten "in the mouth of the black-headed ones (*i.e.*, mankind) "whom his hands have created." In view of this evidence it may be concluded that the description of the creation of mankind had a place in the tablets that are missing; and it is probable that upon another fragment of a tablet[3] we have a copy of the instructions which Marduk was believed to have given to man

---

[1] British Museum, K. 8522. See G. Smith, *Trans. Soc. Bibl. Arch.*, Vol. IV., p. 363, and plates 3 and 4.

[2] The allusion here is to the Fourth Tablet; see above, p. 74.

[3] British Museum, K. 3364.

after his creation. The following extracts from this fragment reveal a very lofty conception of man's duties towards his god and towards his neighbour :—

"Towards thy god shalt thou be pure of heart,
"For that is the glory of the godhead ;
"Prayer and supplication and bowing low to the earth,
"Early in the morning shalt thou offer unto him . . ."

A little further on Marduk continues :—

"The fear of god begets mercy,
"Offerings increase life,
"And prayer absolves from sin.
"He that fears the gods shall not cry aloud [in grief],
"He that fears the Anunnaki[1] shall have a long [life].
"Against friend and neighbour thou shalt not speak [evil].
"Speak not of things that are hidden, [practice] mercy.
"When thou makest a promise (to give), give and [hold] not [back]."

In the hymn which has been referred to in the previous paragraph as having not improbably formed the concluding tablet of the series, the other gods are represented as addressing Marduk, their deliverer, by

[1] *I.e.*, the Spirits of the Earth.

every conceivable name and title of honour. They called him "the life of all the gods," "the god of "pure life," "the bringer of purification," "the god of "the favouring breeze," "the lord of hearing and mercy," "the creator of abundance and mercy, who establishes "plenteousness, and increases all that is small"; and it is also said that when the gods themselves were in sore distress they felt his favouring breeze. The text continues in the above strain, referring to his mercy towards his opponents, his conquest of Tiāmat, and his acts of creation, and Bēl and Ea are made to bestow their own titles upon him. Finally the wise are bidden to ponder on the story, the father is to teach it to his son, and the prince or ruler is to listen to its recital. With such an ode to Marduk as the god of creation the great poem might fitly conclude.

In addition to the great poem, there is reason to believe that several different accounts of the creation were current in Babylonian literature. One such account is preserved on a broken tablet from Ashurbāni-pal's library, which contains a very different description of the great battle with the dragon to that given in the Fourth Tablet of the Creation Series. In this version the fight does not precede the creation of the world but takes place after man has been created and cities built. In fact, men and gods are equally terrified at the dragon's appearance, and it is to deliver the lands from the monster that one of the gods goes out and slays him. The text begins with a description of the terror which came upon creation at the advent of Tiāmat, who has, however, become a male monster, and says :—

"The cities sighed, men [groaned aloud],
"Men uttered lamentation, [they wailed grievously].
"For their lamentation there was none [to help],
"For their grief there was none to take [them by the hand].
"Who was the [great] dragon?
"Tiāmat [1] was the [great] dragon!
"Bēl in heaven has formed [his image].
"Fifty *kasbu* [2] is his length, one *kasbu* [is his breadth],
"Half a rod (?) is his mouth, one rod (?) [his . . .]."

The next few lines continue the description of the dragon, and give the measurements of other parts of his body as being "sixty rods" and "sixty-five rods," and narrate how he wallowed in the water and lashed his tail. All the gods in heaven were afraid. They bowed down and grasped the robe of the Moon-god Sin, and they cried out asking who would go out and slay the monster, and deliver the broad earth, and so make himself king. They then appealed to the god Sukh to undertake the task, but he made excuses. Who

---

[1] Here called *Tāmtu*, "the Sea."
[2] The *kasbu* is a space that can be covered in two hours' travelling; *i.e.*, about six or seven miles.

eventually consented to do battle with the dragon we do not know, for the text is broken, but it is probable that in this version also Marduk was the hero. The end of the composition, in which we find the god, whoever he may have been, setting out to do battle, while one of the other gods cries to him in encouragement, has fortunately been preserved; it reads:—

"'Stir up cloud, storm [and tempest],
"Set the seal of thy life before thy face[1] . . . ,
"And slay the dragon!'
"He stirred up cloud, and storm [and tempest],
"He set the seal of his life before his face . . . ,
"And he slew the dragon.
"For three years and three months, day and [night],
"The blood of the dragon flowed . . ."

The details as to the size of the dragon and the amount of his blood are of considerable interest. In the Creation Series the North wind is said to have carried the blood away into secret places, and the prominence given to the dragon's blood in both versions lends colour to a suggestion that has been made with regard to one of the details in the account of creation given by Berosus. In that version Bēl is said to have formed animals and men from earth mixed with his own blood after one of the gods had, at his command, cut off his head. The account would afford a much closer parallel to the legend as we find it on

---

[1] *I.e.*, as a protection against the monster.

the tablets if we might assume that it was not his own blood, but that of Tiāmat, which Bēl used for the purpose. It is possible that either Polyhistor or Eusebius, or both, misunderstood the original story.

We have described the great story of the creation which was current in Assyria during the seventh century before Christ, as far as its contents can be ascertained from the fragments that have come down to us. The numerous tablets and duplicates inscribed with the legend, which have been found in the ruins of Ashur-bāni-pal's library, indicate the important position it held among the religious and mythological works of the period; and we are right in assuming that this version of the creation was the one most widely accepted during the reigns of the later Assyrian kings. But, although the poem in the form in which we now have it represents the belief most generally held by the Babylonians and Assyrians at this comparatively late period with regard to the manner in which the world came into being, it can only have attained this position gradually. Babylonian literature, in fact, comprises fragments of other myths and legends which give different accounts of the way in which creation took place, and, as one of these is of considerable importance, by reason of the light it throws upon the age and history of such legends in Babylonia, it will be convenient to describe it before considering what connection there may have been between the Babylonian poem and the story of creation in the first chapter of Genesis.

After the great Creation Series the longest, and indeed the only other distinct version of the story of the creation in Babylonian literature now known is found upon one side of a broken incantation-tablet,[1] which was inscribed in the Neo-Babylonian period not earlier than 600 B.C. It was found at Abu-habbah, the site of the ancient city of Sippar in Northern Babylonia, in 1882.

The inscription is of great interest, for it is written in the ancient Sumerian language, and to each line is attached a translation in Semitic Babylonian. The account of the creation here given offers few parallels to the great Creation Series which has been described above. It is true that the god Marduk is credited with the creation of the world, but there is no mention of the battle which the god successfully waged against the powers of chaos before the earth came into being. In fact the god proceeds to the work of creation without any previous struggle and entirely of his own free will. The tablet opens with a description of chaos at a period when the ancient cities and temples of the land had no existence, when no towns had been built, nor any vegetation created—in short, all lands were sea. In the account of the creation that follows it is possible that the order in which the various acts are described

[1] British Museum, No. 82-5-22, 1048.

is not intended to be chronological, but is dictated by the structure of the poem. Otherwise we must assume that the cities of Eridu and Babylon and the temple E-sagil were the things first created, and that their creation preceded not only the construction of the cities of Nippur and Erech and their temples, but even the creation of mankind, and the beasts of the field, and vegetation, and the rivers of Babylonia. Marduk's act of laying a reed, or bank of reeds, upon the waters and creating dust which he poured out round about it would appear to be merely a device for forming dry land in the expanse of waters, and his object in laying in a dam or embankment at the edge of the waters was evidently to keep the sea from flooding the land he had so formed. The text reads as follows:—

"The holy temple, the temple of the gods, in the holy place had not yet been made;
"No reed had sprung up, no tree had been created.
"No brick had been laid, no building had been set up;
"No house had been erected, no city had been built;
"No city had been made, no dwelling-place had been prepared.
"Nippur had not been made, E-kur had not been built;
"Erech had not been created, E-ana had not been built;
"The Deep had not been created, Eridu had not been built;

" Of the pure temple, the temple of the gods, the habitation had not been made.

" All lands were sea.

" At length there was a movement in the sea,

" Then was Eridu made, and E-sagil was built,

" E-sagil, where in the midst of the Deep the god Lugal-dul-azaga dwells.

" The city of Babylon was built, and E-sagil was finished.

" The gods, the Anunnaki, were created at one time;

" The holy city, the dwelling of their hearts' desire, they proclaimed supreme.

" Marduk laid a reed upon the face of the waters,

" He formed dust and poured it out upon the reed.

" That he might cause the gods to dwell in the habitation of their hearts' desire,

" He formed mankind.

" The goddess Aruru together with him created the seed of mankind.

" He formed the beasts of the field and the cattle of the field.

" He created the Tigris, and the Euphrates, and he set them in their place,

" Their names he declared to be good.

" The *ushshu*-plant, the *dittu*-plant of the marsh, the reed and the forest he created,

" The lands, and the marshes, and the swamps;

THE CREATION OF MEN AND CITIES. 91

" The wild cow and her young, that is the wild ox;
the ewe and her young, that is the lamb of the
fold;
" Plantations and forests;
" The he-goat, and the mountain-goat, and the . . .
" The lord Marduk laid in a dam by the side of the
sea,
" .   . as before he had not made,
" .   .   . . he brought into existence.
" . . . . trees he created,
" [Bricks] he made in their place.
" . . . . . . brickwork he made;
" [Houses he made], cities he built;
" [Cities he made], dwelling-places he prepared.
" [Nippur he made], E-kur he built;
" [Erech he made], E-ana he built."

The rest of the legend is broken off, and the reverse of the tablet does not contain a continuation of the legend, but a prayer, or incantation, which was to be recited for the purification of the temple E-zida in Borsippa. The connection between the legend and the incantation is not obvious, but the fact that the legend is found upon an incantation tablet does not detract from its value, and does not indicate a late date for its composition. In fact, as will presently be pointed out, there are grounds for believing that the legend may go back to a time when Sumerian was still a living language, and when it was not merely a dead tongue employed in religious ritual and known only to the scribes.

In this connection mention must be made of two tablets, which are frequently said to contain the "Cuthæan legend of Creation," and have been thought to describe a local account of the creation which was current in the ancient city of Cuthah. It has been asserted that this legend gives an account of the creation of the world by Nergal, the god of Cuthah, after he had conquered the brood of monsters which Tiāmat had brought forth. Recently, however, it has been pointed out[1] that the tablets are not concerned with the creation, but with the fortunes of an early Babylonian king. In the reign of this king, whose name is unknown, the land was invaded by a strange race of monsters who were descended from the gods, and for three years the king waged war against this foe unsuccessfully, but at length he defeated them. In fact, the tablets have nothing whatever to do with the creation or with the fight between Tiāmat and the gods; but, as the two tablets which contain this story have been regarded as fragments of a legend of the creation, it will perhaps be well to give a translation of them. The words of the text are put in the mouth of the king himself, who throughout speaks in the first person; the beginnings of both the tablets are missing, but where the text

---

[1] See Zimmern, *Zeitschrift für Assyriologie*, Bd. XII. (1898), pp. 317 ff.

becomes continuous we find a description of the strange monsters, which had invaded the land, in the following words:—

"A people who drink turbid water, and who drink not pure water,

"Whose sense is perverted, have taken (men) captive, have triumphed over them, and have committed slaughter.

"On a tablet nought is written, nought is left (to write).[1] In mine own person

"I went not forth, I did not give them battle.

"A people who have the bodies of birds of the hollow, men who have the faces of ravens,

"Did the great gods create.

"In the ground the gods created a dwelling for them,

"Tiāmat gave them suck,

"The lady of the gods brought them into the world.

"In the midst of the mountain (of the world), they became strong, they waxed great, they multiplied exceedingly.

"Seven kings, brethren, fair and comely,

"360,000 in number were their warriors,

"Banini, their father, was king; their mother, Melili, queen.

"Their eldest brother, their leader, was named Memangab,

[1] *I.e.*, the city was in confusion, and no business was transacted, and no records kept.

"Their second brother was named Medudu."

The tablet then gives the names of the other five brethren, all of which are, however, broken. After the names a gap occurs in the legend, for the beginning of the second column of the principal tablet is missing. Where the story is again connected we find the king had enquired of the gods if he should give the enemy battle. He addressed them through his priests, and offered up to them offerings of lambs, which he placed in rows of seven. The answer of the gods was evidently favourable, for he decided to engage the enemy; but for a space of three years every man he sent against the foe was destroyed. The text continues:—

"As the first year drew near,

"120,000 warriors I sent out, but not one of them returned alive.

"As the second year drew near,

"90,000 warriors I sent out, but not one of them returned alive.

"As the third year drew near,

"60,700 warriors I sent out, but not one returned alive.

"Despairing, powerless, perishing, I was full of woe, and I groaned aloud,

"And said I to my heart: 'By my life!

"What have I brought upon my realm!

"I am a king, who hath brought no prosperity to his country,

"And a shepherd, who hath brought no prosperity
   to his people.
" But this thing will I do. In mine own person
   will I go forth!
" The pride of the people of the night I will curse
   with death and destruction,
" With fear, terror, . . . and famine,
" . . . and with misery of every kind!' "

The king then foretold the destruction of his enemies by means, apparently, of a deluge, and before setting out to meet them he again offered up offerings to the gods. How he conquered the enemy we do not know, but the fact that he went forth in his own person to do battle against them evidently secured for him the favour of the gods, and victory over the monstrous creatures who had so long oppressed his land. In the latter portion of the legend the king addresses words of encouragement to any future prince who shall rule over his kingdom. The king exhorts his successor when in peril, not to despair, but to take courage from his own example, in the following words :—

" Thou, O king, or ruler, or prince, or any one
   whatsoever,
" Whom the god shall call to rule over the kingdom,
" A tablet concerning these matters have I made for
   thee, and a record have I written for thee.
" In the city of Cuthah, in the temple E-shidlam,
" In the shrine of Nergal have I deposited it for thee.

"Behold this record, and
"To the words thereof hearken,
"That thou mayest not despair, nor be feeble,
"That thou mayest not fear, nor be affrighted.
"Stablish thyself firmly,
"Sleep in peace beside thy wife,
"Strengthen thy walls,
"Fill thy trenches with water,
"Bring in thy treasure-chests, and thy corn, and thy silver, and thy goods, and thy possessions,
"[And thy weapons], and thy household stuff."

The ruler himself is bidden to take heed unto his own safety, not to go forth nor to draw near his foe. The meaning of the exhortation seems to be that as in days of old the gods helped the king of the land and turned his mourning into victory, so in the future when the land is in sore trouble and the foe is at the gate the king is not to despair but to expect that the gods will help him also.

This legend has for some years been known as "the Cuthæan legend of Creation," but from the above translation it will be seen that the description is inaccurate. It was thought that the poem was spoken by the god Nergal, who was supposed to be waging war against the brood of Tiâmat, and it was assumed that Nergal took the place of Marduk in accordance with local tradition at Cuthah. It is clear, however, that although the tablet on which the legend was inscribed

NOT A CREATION LEGEND.

was meant to be preserved at Cuthah in the shrine of Nergal (as stated towards the end of the poem) the speaker is not the god Nergal but an old Babylonian king; and we have already seen that this king recounts how the gods delivered him and his land from the hosts of the monsters. It is true that in the description of the monsters, some of which had the bodies of birds and others the heads of ravens, Tiāmat is mentioned as having suckled them; but this statement hardly affords sufficient evidence to justify their identification with her monster brood which has already been described in the Creation story. It is more probable that Tiāmat is called their foster-mother in order to indicate their terrible nature. Moreover, the speaker in the poem does not perform any acts of creation, but does battle with the monsters merely to deliver his land from their assault.

In conclusion it may be mentioned that last year a fragment of a Babylonian tablet preserved in the Imperial Ottoman Museum at Constantinople was published,[1] which contains part of a copy of this legend; the inscription upon it is a parallel and not a duplicate text. If, as has been stated, this fragment belongs to the old Babylonian period, it will afford valuable evidence of the early existence of these legends in Babylonia.

The great Babylonian legend of creation has been

---

[1] See Scheil, *Recueil de Travaux*, Vol. XX., p. 65 f.

examined and its variant forms have been traced, so far as they can be restored from late Assyrian and Babylonian tablets, and from the extract from the history of Berosus which has come down to us. Not one of the tablets on which the legends are written belongs to a period earlier than the seventh century B.C., and the question naturally arises, Do the legends they contain also date from the seventh century, or must they be referred to some earlier period? In other words, Were they composed by the priestly scribes who had them written upon the actual tablets which we possess, or did these scribes simply copy the documents belonging to an older period? And, if the scribes of the seventh century were mere copyists and not composers, we must also ask, To what period must we assign the origin of the old texts which they copied? These questions can, fortunately, be decided by a careful examination of the available evidence.

The first question is best answered by considering the various forms which the Creation legends assume on different tablets. Were the legends brand-new compositions of the seventh century we should expect to find all the copies which were written at the same time and preserved in the same library agreeing closely with each other. It is true that we do find several copies of the Creation tablets which correspond with each other word for word, and these were, no doubt, made from some common archetype. But we also possess another tablet from Ashur-bāni-pal's library, which gives quite a different account of the struggle with Tiāmat. The tablet has been already referred to,[1] and we have seen that on it the fight is described as taking place after and not before creation, and that Tiāmat's body is not used to form the vault of heaven; moreover, the dragon is a male and not a female monster, and the description of it is quite different from that in the Creation Series; and finally another god than Anu is first of all asked to go forth and slay her. Other events differently described may have been narrated on the tablet, for only a fragment of it has been preserved; but those that we have enumerated are sufficient to prove our point. Such variant forms of the same story cannot have arisen in one generation. They presuppose many centuries of tradition, during which the two accounts were handed down independently. Though the two stories were derived from a common original, they were related in different cities in different ways. At first they were probably identical in form, but in course of time variations crept in, and two or more forms of the story were developed along different lines. The process must have been gradual, and the resultant forms of the story afford sufficient evidence as to the great age of their common ancestor. That they were found together in Ashur-bāni-pal's library is to be explained as the result of that monarch's energy

[1] See pp. 84 ff.

in scouring the country for literary and religious works.

A similar conclusion follows if we compare the two separate and distinct versions of the creation which have also been described above.[1] In both of them Marduk is the creator of the world, but, while the great Creation Series is chiefly taken up with the revolt and conquest of Tiāmat as a necessary preliminary to the creation of the world, in the shorter Sumerian version there is no trace of such a conflict, nor is the dragon Tiāmat even mentioned. In this tablet we have an instance of quite a different version of the creation which we may perhaps assume goes back to a period when the dragon-myth had not become associated with the creation of the world. The so-called "Cuthæan legend of Creation" cannot be cited as a true variant form of the legend, for, as we have seen, it is not a creation legend at all, but a story of an old Babylonian king. It contains a reference to the dragon Tiāmat, however, and evidently presupposes on the part of the reader a knowledge of the story concerning the monsters to which she is said to have given birth. If the fragmentary duplicate of the inscription which has recently been found[2] was written in the old Babylonian period, this reference to Tiāmat in the legend is important evidence for the early date of the dragon-myth. But,

---

[1] *I.e.*, the great Creation Series on pp. 61 ff., and the Sumerian version of the Creation on pp. 88 ff.

[2] See p. 97.

EVIDENCE FROM SCULPTURE. 101

even if we leave the Cuthæan tablet out of account altogether, the existence of the two versions of the Creation story and the variants we have traced in the accounts of the fight with Tiămat prove conclusively their early origin.

So far we have considered the internal evidence of date offered by the legends themselves. Additional evidence, pointing in the same direction, is afforded by a study of certain aspects of Babylonian and Assyrian art. In a temple built by Ashur-nātsir-pal at Nimrūd, the site of the ancient Assyrian city of Calah, there was found a slab sculptured in relief with a representation of the fight between Marduk and Tiămat.[1] The monster, half bird, half lion, turns roaring in anger towards the god who, in human form and borne upon four wings, swoops down to give battle. Now Ashur-nātsir-pal reigned from B.C. 884 to B.C. 860, so that we here have evidence of the existence of the legend more than two hundred years before the formation of the library of Ashur-bāni-pal, who reigned from B.C. 669 to about B.C. 625. Moreover the battle between Marduk and Tiămat was a very favourite subject for engraving upon cylinder-seals. Numbers of these have been found, and many give quite different representations of Tiămat. The god Marduk is generally represented in human form with wings, but the

---

[1] In the British Museum, Nimroud Gallery, Nos. 28 and 29. See the illustration on p. 75.

monster assumes many guises. Sometimes she is pictured as a winged and human-headed lion, at other times she has the body of a horse or bull, and the wings and crested head of a bird. On certain cylinder-seals she figures simply as a beast, while on others though she has an animal's body she has a woman's head.[1] On a very interesting cylinder, here published

The god Marduk armed with the thunderbolt and other weapons standing on the back of Tiāmat and slaying her. (From a cylinder-seal in the British Museum, No. 89,589.)

for the first time, she is represented as a huge dragon on whose back the god Marduk, fully armed, has leapt, and he and his ministers are in the act of slaying her. It is true that many of these cylinder-seals belong to the late Assyrian and Persian periods, *i.e.*, from about B.C. 700 to B.C. 300; a few, however, are archaic in style and may be assigned to a somewhat earlier date. But without laying too much stress on the possibly early date of some of them, the great variety

[1] For reproductions of several cylinder-seals of this class, see the *Collection de Clercq*, Plates xxix. ff.

EVIDENCE FROM HISTORICAL INSCRIPTIONS. 103

of treatment of the same subject which they present certainly points to the existence of many variant forms of the legend, and so indirectly bears witness to its early origin.

A third class of evidence for the early date of the legends of creation may be found in certain passages in the historical inscriptions which record the erection of statues and the making of temple furniture, etc., in the earlier periods of Babylonian history. In the copy of an inscription of Agum, an early Babylonian king, who flourished not later than the seventeenth century before Christ, we have, fortunately, an allusion to the dragon-myth of Babylonia. Now although we do not possess an actual inscription of this king's reign, the copy of one in the British Museum, which, we know, was made for Ashur-bāni-pal,[1] is to all intents and purposes just as good. From this we learn that Agum brought back to Babylon a statue of the god Marduk and one of the goddess Tsarpanitum, which at some previous time had been carried off to the land of Khanī which lay to the north-west of Babylonia. The statues were carried to the temple E-sagil in Babylon, and with much pomp and ceremony were re-installed in their shrines. Agum recounts at length the sumptuous temple furniture which he caused to be made for this occasion, and also the

[1] Published in *Cuneiform Inscriptions of Western Asia*, Vol. V., plate 33.

apparel and head-dresses for the statues of these gods, which he caused to be made of fine gold and inlaid with precious stones. In the shrine itself, he tells us, he also set a dragon, which must have resembled those made at a later time by Nebuchadnezzar and Neriglissar,[1] and that this dragon was connected with Tiāmat of the Creation legend is clear from the fact that along with her he also set up figures of monsters, including vipers, and monsters called *lakhmu*, and a ram, and a hurricane, and a raging hound, and a fish-man, and a goat-fish. The list of the eleven classes of monsters in the Creation Series gives us monster-serpents, and monster-vipers, and a viper, and a dragon, and monsters called *lakhamu*, and a hurricane, and a raging hound, and a scorpion-man, and tempests, and a fish-man, and rams. We are not here concerned with the astrological character of these monsters, nor with their connection with the origin of the signs of the Zodiac; but what is evident from the two lists is that already in the time of Agum the legend of Tiāmat and her monster brood had been accepted and had become absorbed into the ancient religious traditions of the land.

A further reference to the legend may be seen in

[1] When Nebuchadnezzar II. set up colossal serpents in the gateways of Babylon in the sixth century before Christ, and when Neriglissar, his successor, set up eight such serpents which he had made of bronze and coated with silver, it is tolerably clear that these figures were intended to represent the dragon of the Creation story.

the mention of another object used for ceremonial purposes which was given by Agum to Marduk's temple. In Marduk's shrine, beside the great serpent he set what he terms a *tāmtu*, or "sea"; this was, no doubt, a large basin, or "laver," similar to the brazen sea of Solomon's temple which stood upon twelve oxen.[1] Such a vessel, as its name indicates, was symbolical of the abyss of water personified in the legend by Apsū and Tiāmat, and its mention in the inscription in such close connection with the dragon and the brood of monsters is peculiarly significant. Similar vessels, called *apsē, i.e.,* "abysses," or "deeps," as we know from other inscriptions, were placed in the temples of Babylonia from the earliest periods. Bur-Sin, a king of Ur who lived about B.C. 2500, erected for the god Enki, or Ea, a *zu-ab ki-ag-ga-ni*, "an abyss "that was dear to him";[2] and in the reign of Ur-Ninā, an ancient Sumerian king of Shirpurla, and one of the earliest rulers of that city whose names have come down to us, such vessels were already used in religious ceremonies. The latter monarch caused a limestone tablet to be inscribed with the list of the temples erected during his reign, and in the inscription upon it we read that he constructed a *zu-ab gal*, or "great "abyss."[3]

[1] 1 Kings vii. 23 ff.
[2] The tablet containing this record is published in *Cun. Inscr. of West. Asia*, Vol. I., plate 3, No. XII. (1).
[3] See De Sarzec, *Découvertes en Chaldée*, plate II., No. 1, Col. III., l. 5 f.

The fact that at these early periods Ur-Ninā and Bur-Sin provided their temples with "seas" and "deeps," *i.e.*, lavers, does not, of course, prove that the Creation legends were current among the Sumerians in the forms in which we find them on Assyrian tablets of the seventh century before Christ. But the references at least indicate the source and period to which the legends may be traced. The Semitic Babylonians learnt from the Sumerians the art of writing; in their business transactions they adopted the legal forms and phrases that were current in the land before they came there, while as for the gods of the conquered race they either adopted them or identified them with their own deities. It is probable, therefore, that from the Sumerians also they took their ideas of the creation of the world. We know that at the time of Khammurabi the Semitic scribes copied out and studied Sumerian religious texts, and from the ancient libraries of Southern Babylonia we have recovered religious compositions bearing a striking resemblance to those which were employed in the Assyrian temples of the later period; but in this early Sumerian literature we have not yet found any fragment of the story of the creation, or indeed of any mythological legend. The shorter version of the creation inscribed upon a Neo-Babylonian tablet is, however, written in Sumerian and furnished with a Semitic translation; and, although the scribes of that late period, in all probability, frequently attempted to compose in the Sumerian language, that version of the Creation story may well have been copied from an early original Sumerian document. As the study of the Sumerian language progresses and the mass of tablets that have been brought to light within the last few years are examined and published, we may in time find definite proofs of the existence of such legends. Meanwhile the evidence available is sufficient to show that the legends of the creation current in Assyria and Babylonia during the seventh and succeeding centuries before Christ were based upon archetypes the existence of which may date from Sumerian times. The actual text of the legends, no doubt, underwent many processes of editing; the division of the great poem into sections, each written on a separate tablet, may well have been the work of later scribes; but the legends themselves were ancient and had their origin in the earliest period of Babylonian history.

We have now described the contents of the great Babylonian poem of the creation, we have referred to the variant traditions that have come down to us concerning the several episodes of the story, and we have also examined a second version of the creation which bears but small resemblance to the great poem. We have suggested that the existence of so many variants is a proof of the great age of the legends, and it has been seen that this evidence is corroborated by the traces which the legends have left in Babylonian and

Assyrian art, and by certain indirect references to them in some early historical inscriptions. The extracts given from the tablets will have conveyed better than any summary would have done the exact nature of their contents, and, as the translations have been made as literal as possible, the reader has been able to form his own opinion as to the nature of the resemblance which may be detected between these ancient Babylonian stories and the account of the creation in the Book of Genesis. It now remains to consider what connection there is between the Hebrew and the Babylonian accounts of the creation of the world.

That there must have been a connection between the two accounts is generally admitted, for it is only necessary to read the tablets to be struck by their resemblance to the Biblical narrative in many particulars; the question now to be decided is, In what does this connection consist? Three possible solutions of the problem suggest themselves: (1) The Babylonians may have derived their legends from the Hebrews; (2) both Babylonians and Hebrews, as different branches of the same Semitic race, may have inherited the legends from a common ancestral stock; and (3) the Hebrews may have derived their legends from Babylonia. Of these possible solutions the first may be dismissed at once. During whatever period of their history the inhabitants of Mesopotamia came in contact with the peoples of the Mediterranean coast, they always came in the character of conquerors, and we know from their inscriptions that the Babylonians and Assyrians regarded the other nations of Western Asia only in the light of payers of tribute. It is inconceivable, therefore, that they should have borrowed their sacred traditions from a race they considered inferior to themselves; moreover, the existence of the legends in Babylonia has been traced to a very early period, before any contact between the Babylonians and the Hebrews can have taken place. The second theory has far more to recommend it, and has met with warm supporters. It has been urged that, coming of the same stock, both Babylonians and Hebrews possessed the legends of the creation as a common inheritance, and that each of these nations modified and developed them independently. Against this explanation is to be set the distinctly Babylonian character and colouring of the stories, and it is generally regarded as impossible for them to have other than a Babylonian origin. In the account of the Flood given in Genesis, which will be referred to in the following chapter, the Babylonian origin is still more apparent. We are, therefore, reduced to the third solution as being the most probable of the three. The legends, we may conclude, are Babylonian in origin and character, and the resemblances which the account in Genesis bears to them must, we think, be put down to Babylonian influence. We may then ask, At what time, and by what means, was this influence exerted which has left its traces on the Hebrew story in Genesis?

The critical study of the text of Genesis has shown that this book, like the rest of the Pentateuch, is not from the pen of a single writer, and that it is made up of a number of separate works. In the earlier periods of Hebrew history these works had not been woven into a continuous narrative, and they were not in the form in which they are now known to us; each work had a separate existence. The evidence on which this conclusion rests consists in part of the numerous repetitions which occur throughout the books, and in the existence of two separate and sometimes quite different narratives of the same event, and in difficulties in chronology, and the like. A careful study of the Hebrew text by scholars throughout the present century [1] has further shown that there are three principal works on which the Pentateuch and the Book of Joshua are based. These works dealt with the early history of the Hebrew race, and, as each of them frequently goes over the same ground as the others, it is easy to explain the repetitions which the combined narrative contains. Each of these books, or histories, can be recognized with tolerable certainty by their differences in style and treatment, the use of phrases peculiar to themselves, the names for God which they

---

[1] Cf. Cheyne, *Founders of Old Testament Criticism: Biographical, Descriptive, and Critical Studies* (London, 1893).

employ, etc. One of these works was used to form the groundwork of the "Hexateuch," or first six books of the Bible, and it was well adapted for the purpose, inasmuch as it presented an orderly system of chronology. It dealt with the laws and customs of the people, and explained their origin; and from the general nature of its contents it is usually termed the "Priestly writing," or the "Priests' code." The other two books which were incorporated with this "Priestly writing," dealt with the legends and early history of the Hebrew race; they are far more primitive and picturesque in style than the more formal and annalistic narrative with which they are combined. The writers of these two narratives are generally distinguished by the names "Jehovist" and "Elohist," from the fact that in one of them the Divine name employed is Jahweh or Jehovah, translated as "the Lord" in the Authorized Version; while in the other it is Elōhīm, which is translated as "God."

It is needless for our purpose to discuss here the relations which these three works bear to one another, or to enumerate any additional documents of which use was made in the Hexateuch. It will suffice to state that in the early chapters of Genesis, two only, of the three writings referred to, have been used —the "Priestly writing"[1] and the "Jehovistic

---

[1] The "Priestly writing" also makes use of the word Elōhīm for "God."

narrative."[1] Thus the account of the creation in Genesis i. 1—ii. 4 (first half of the verse) is from the former writing, and contains a complete account of the history of creation in a series of successive acts. The story of the garden of Eden, which follows in chapters ii. 4 (second half of the verse)—iii. 24, is taken from the "Jehovistic narrative," and it gives another account of creation which is not marked by the literary precision and balanced structure of the first chapter. That account had given a complete description of the making of the world; the second narrative begins at the beginning again, going back to a time when there were no plants, nor beasts, nor men, and then narrates their creation. If we compare these accounts with the two principal traditions of the creation preserved in Babylonian literature, and which we have already described,[2] we see that the account in the first chapter agrees more closely with the longer Babylonian narrative than with the shorter; on the other hand the earlier part of the story of the garden of Eden, both in its structure and in several of its phrases, is not unlike the shorter Babylonian version.

To the greater part of the story of the garden of Eden, no parallel has been found in Babylonian

---

[1] An analysis of the first eleven chapters of the Book of Genesis on these lines is given in Prof. Driver's *Introduction to the Literature of the Old Testament*, (6th ed.), pp. 14 ff.

[2] See above, pp. 61 ff., and 88 ff.

THE GARDEN OF EDEN.

mythology; it has, however, been pointed out that in the description of Paradise Babylonian sources have been largely drawn upon. The illustration here given has been by some supposed to be a Babylonian representation of the story of the temptation of Eve; but as no cuneiform text in support of this view has been forthcoming, the identification of the female figure

[Impression of a cylinder-seal representing a male and a female figure seated near a sacred tree; behind the woman is a serpent. (British Museum, No. 89,326.)

with Eve must be regarded as somewhat fanciful. Writers on Babylonian mythology have sought to find in the Babylonian legends the counterparts of Adam and Eve, but without success. Recently Ea-bani, a mythical and savage hero of the Gilgamesh legend,[1] has been identified with Adam, and the maiden Ukhat, by whom he was tempted, with Eve,[2] but the grounds on which the identifications are made are not convincing.

In consequence of the many points of identity between the Hebrew and the Babylonian versions of

[1] See below, pp. 150 ff.
[2] See Jastrow, *Amer. Jour. Semit. Lang.*, Vol. XV., No. 4 (July, 1899).

the creation, some advanced critics hold that the Jews heard the Babylonian stories for the first time during their exile in Babylon, and that on their return from captivity they brought them back with them and incorporated them in their sacred writings. Against this assumption it has been urged that it is hardly likely the captive Jews would have adopted strange legends from their conquerors, and raised them to a place of honour among their national traditions. But, apart from this consideration, such an assumption is not necessary in order to explain the resemblances—indeed it is hardly admissible, for it takes no account of the striking differences and variations which the narratives present. Moreover, in many passages throughout the Old Testament, we find traces of the Babylonian dragon-myth, and it is scarcely possible that all such references should date from the post-exilic period.

In several passages we find allusions to a dragon or serpent who is thought to inhabit the deep. Thus the prophet Amos, describing how none shall escape God's hands when He comes in judgment, exclaims, "And though they hide themselves in the top of "Carmel, I will search and take them out thence; "and though they be hid from my sight in the bottom "of the sea, thence will I command the serpent, and "he shall bite them."[1] This serpent or dragon is sometimes referred to as "Leviathan" or "Rahab,"

---

[1] Amos ix. 3.

and in several passages allusion is made to a battle with the dragon of the deep, in which the dragon was pierced or slain. "Awake, awake, put on strength, "O arm of the Lord; awake, as in the days of old, "the generations of ancient times. Art thou not it "that cut Rahab in pieces, that pierced the dragon?"[1] Here the allusion to a battle with a dragon, that took place "in days of old," is unmistakable. "Thou didst "divide" (Heb. "break up") "the sea by thy strength: "thou brakest the heads of the dragons in the waters. "Thou brakest the heads of leviathan in pieces, "thou gavest him to be meat to the people inhabiting "the wilderness."[2] In this and in the following passage from the Book of Job the connection of the dragon with the deep is brought out:[3] "He stirreth "up the sea with his power, and by his understanding "he smiteth through Rahab. By his spirit the heavens "are garnished; his hand has pierced the swift serpent."[4] In the last sentence quoted the parallelism between the garnishing of the heavens and the piercing of the serpent recalls the Babylonian myth, in which Marduk formed the heavens from half of the dragon's body. A phrase in an earlier chapter of Job appears to reflect another episode of the Babylonian legend; in the course of a description of the power of God in comparison with man's impotence it is stated: "God will

---

[1] Isaiah li. 9.   [2] Psalm lxxiv. 13 f.
[3] See also Psalm lxxxix. 9 f.   [4] Job xxvi. 12 f.

"not withdraw his anger; the helpers of Rahab do "stoop under him."[1] The "helpers of Rahab," stooping beneath their conqueror, call to mind "the gods, her "helpers," who went at the side of Tiāmat, and shared her defeat.

It is doubtful if the Babylonian form of the name Rahab has been found in a synonym employed for the dragon on one of the creation fragments,[2] but at least the conception and description of the monster may be regarded as based on the Babylonian myth. Egypt is sometimes referred to as Rahab,[3] but this application of the term does not conflict with its Babylonian origin. The origin of the kindred monster "Behemoth" may, on the other hand, be rightly traced to Egypt, for many of the characteristics assigned to him in Job xl. 15 ff., are evidently taken from the hippopotamus; while the picture of Leviathan, which immediately follows that of Behemoth, offers a distinct contrast to it, and would not be inappropriate as a description of the monster Tiāmat. In the passages cited above a dragon-myth is clearly and unmistakably referred to. The passages are poetical, and the language is to a great extent figurative and symbolical; the figures and symbols employed, however, are drawn from mythology, and presuppose a knowledge of the legend. Traces of the myth may perhaps also be seen

---

[1] Job ix. 13.   [2] See Gunkel's *Schöpfung und Chaos*, pp. 29 and 418.
[3] See Psalm lxxxvii. 4, and Isaiah xxx. 7.

in certain phrases or expressions, as in Gen. xlix. 25, where the expression "the deep that coucheth beneath" seems to suggest the picture of a beast about to spring. But it is very easy to press imagery too far, and to see mythological references in pictures suggested to the poet by his own observations of nature. If, however, we select only those passages in the Old Testament, in which the dragon-myth is definitely referred to, we have sufficient evidence to show that the myth must have been familiar to the Hebrews long before the exile.

It now remains to enquire at what period before the exile these legends from Babylon could have reached the Hebrews. The question is one that does not admit of any certain or definite answer, but it is permissible at least to search for any evidence on which a conjectural theory may be based. Such evidence is furnished by one of the most surprising discoveries of Babylonian tablets that has been made during recent years. In 1887 at Tell el-Amarna, a village in Upper Egypt on the east bank of the Nile, the natives unearthed about three-hundred-and-twenty clay tablets inscribed in the Babylonian character. The ruins near the village mark the site of a town that was built by Khu-en-aten, or Amenophis IV., who was king of Egypt about B.C. 1500. The finding of these Babylonian tablets on Egyptian soil was of the greatest historical interest, and has considerably modified the notions generally held up to the time of their discovery with regard to the early influence of Babylonia upon the other nations of the nearer East. An examination of the tablets showed that some were letters and drafts of letters that passed between the kings of Egypt, Amenophis III. and IV., and contemporary kings of countries and districts of Western Asia; others proved to be letters and reports addressed by princes and governors of cities in Palestine, Phœnicia, and Syria to the King of Egypt. It is not necessary for our present purpose to give a detailed description of the contents of these documents, and it will suffice to point to the evidence which they furnish of the far-reaching influence of Babylonian culture during the XVth century B.C. That correspondence between kings of Assyria, or Babylon, and Egypt should be conducted in the Babylonian language is not so very surprising, but that governors of Egyptian cities and provinces on the Mediterranean coast should make their reports in the same tongue shows that a knowledge of Babylonian was common throughout Western Asia, and that the Babylonian language, like French at the present day, was at this period the language of diplomacy. It is obvious that the Babylonian literature must have found its way among the nations that used its language, and that this was the case there is conclusive evidence among the Tell el-Amarna tablets themselves. Two of these documents, in fact, are not letters or reports, but relate to Babylonian legends, one containing a legend concerning the goddess Ereshkigal, the other inscribed with the legend of Adapa.[1] It is clear, therefore, that the legends of Babylon were known to the Egyptians of this time and the inference is justified that the tribes of Syria and the Mediterranean coast must have also been acquainted with them. We may conclude, therefore, that the Babylonian legends of creation had penetrated to Canaan long before the immigration of the Israelites, and, as the Israelites after the conquest of the country had close intercourse with its previous inhabitants, it is not improbable that they received from them many of the legends and myths, which they in their turn had derived from Babylon.

It has even been suggested that the Hebrews of a still earlier time, during the patriarchal period, may have acquired the legends by direct contact with Babylonia. Tradition held that Terah, the ancestor of the Israelites, had dwelt in Ur of the Chaldees,[2] which is now generally identified with the city of Ur in Southern Babylonia, and it is urged that Abraham, Terah's son, when migrating from Mesopotamia to Canaan may have carried with him the legends of the land of his nativity. If this were so, however, we should expect to find more frequent references to them among the earlier literature of the Hebrews, and it seems to be more probable that the acquisition of the legends should be assigned to a time subsequent to the conquest of Canaan. At some

[1] See below, pp. 188 ff.   [2] Gen. xi. 28.

unknown period, then, whether by inheritance from the Canaanites or by contact with Babylonia itself, we may assume that the Hebrews acquired the Babylonian legends which we find incorporated in their national traditions. In the absence of any positive information one point, at least, is clear, that is to say, the Jews of the exile did not come across Babylonian mythology as an entirely new and unfamiliar subject, much of which they adopted and modified on their return to Jerusalem. It is possible that their sojourn in Babylon during the captivity may have given an impetus to their study of the Babylonian elements in their own traditions, but the wide differences which these present to the forms of the corresponding legends that have been recovered in the cuneiform inscriptions forbid the supposition that they were directly borrowed at this period. In the apocryphal story of the destruction of the great dragon in Babylon by Daniel we doubtless have a late reproduction of the Babylonian myth, and the contrast this narrative presents to the Biblical stories of creation is singularly instructive. From the absence in the latter of all grotesque and mythological detail, from the monotheism which is strictly in accord with the teaching of the prophets before the exile, we may infer that the stories had long been familiar in Israel, and that Ezra and the Jews of the restoration did not compose these narratives but were compilers of earlier traditions of their race.

CHAPTER IV.

THE STORY OF THE DELUGE.

IN the traditions of many races scattered in various parts of the world is to be found a story, under many different forms and with many variations, of a great flood or deluge which in former times inundated and laid waste the land in which they dwelt. The explanation that such traditions refer to a universal deluge which took place in the early ages of the world, is now generally regarded as inadmissible, inasmuch as there is no trace of such a catastrophe in the earth's geological formation. Moreover science has shown that in the present physical condition of the world such a universal deluge would be impossible. It is not necessary on the other hand to refer all these scattered legends to the direct influence of the Biblical story of the flood. Primitive races, dwelling in low-lying and well-watered districts, in their conflict with nature meet with no more destructive foe than inundation, and amongst such races it would be surprising if we did not find stories of past floods from which but few dwellers in the land escaped. It is probable, however, that the story of the flood in Genesis is responsible for some of the deluge legends, though it is now certain that the Biblical story itself is not original, but was derived from a similar legend of the Babylonians.

From the extracts that have been preserved of the history of Berosus [1] we obtain a brief summary of the Babylonian version of the deluge. According to this account, ten Babylonian kings reigned before the deluge, which occurred in the reign of a king named Xisuthros. To this king the god Chronos appeared in a vision and warned him that a flood would take place which would destroy mankind. The god therefore bade him write a history of the world from the beginning, and place it in Sippar, the city of the sun; he was then to build a ship into which he might bring his friends and relations, and every kind of bird and beast. Xisuthros did as the god told him, and the flood came upon the earth. After the flood had begun to abate, Xisuthros sent out birds from the vessel to see if the waters had fallen, but as they found no resting-place they returned. After some days he again sent them out, and this time they came back with mud upon their feet. The third time he sent them out they did not return. He therefore came forth from the vessel, with his wife, his daughter, and the pilot, and upon the side

---

[1] See Eusebius, *Chron.* I., ed. Schoene, col. 20 ff.

of the mountain upon which the ship was stranded he offered a sacrifice, and immediately he and his three companions were taken up into heaven. Those who had remained in the ship then came forth, and as they could not find Xisuthros they lamented and called on him by name. He did not appear to them, however, though they heard his voice telling them that he and his companions were now living with the gods. Xisuthros further informed them that the land they were in was called Armenia, and he told them to return to Babylonia and to search for and recover the writings hidden at Sippar. Those that were left carried out his instructions, and found the writings and built cities; and thus Babylon was again inhabited.

This legend preserved from the history of Berosus was long supposed to have taken its colouring from the account in Genesis, but it is now admitted that Berosus derived the story from Babylonian sources. On the tablets from Ashur-bāni-pal's library a very complete form of the legend has been recovered. These tablets date from the seventh century B.C., and the story told on them appears as part of a great poem concerning an ancient hero named Gilgamesh. The poem was divided into twelve sections, each of which was written upon a separate tablet; these are described in detail in the following chapter. It must here suffice to point out that many of the stories comprised in the poem have no organic connection with the original legend of the hero. Gilgamesh was the most prominent heroic figure in Babylonian mythology, and, as with many heroes of the past, his name has formed a centre around which stories and legends of quite distinct origin have gathered in the course of time. One such legend is the story of the deluge which occurs on the Eleventh Tablet of the series. The story, of which we give a translation, loses nothing by being taken from its context. It there forms a complete tale related to Gilgamesh by Tsīt-napishtim, who together with his family was saved from the deluge. That the legend had originally no connection with the story of Gilgamesh is sufficiently clear from the artificial manner of its introduction, but, if further proof were needed, it has recently been supplied by the discovery of a broken Babylonian tablet, which contains a version of the story as it was told at an early period of Babylonian history.

The tablet is dated in the reign of Ammizaduga, one of the last kings of the First Dynasty of Babylon, and may therefore be roughly ascribed to about B.C. 2100. It was found during the excavations that were recently undertaken by the Turkish Government at Abu-Habbah, the site of the ancient city of Sippar, and no doubt it represents the local form of the legend that was current in that city during this early period. The tablet is unfortunately very badly preserved, but from what remains of it, it is quite certain that it has been inscribed with a variant account of the story of the deluge. Even at this time the story was not a short one, for the text is written in eight columns, four on each side of the tablet. In the second column of the tablet a god appears to be giving directions for sending destruction upon men, while in the seventh column, towards the end of the tablet, the god Ea remonstrates with this deity for sending the deluge and destroying mankind; in the last line but one of the text, moreover, the name Atrakhāsis occurs.[1] So little has been preserved of the tablet, however, that its chief interest is derived from the note, or colophon, with which it concludes. From this we learn two very important facts: (1) the name of the composition of which the tablet forms a part, and (2) the date at which the tablet was written. With regard to the first of these points we find that the story is not described as the Eleventh Tablet of the poem of Gilgamesh, but as the Second Tablet of quite a different composition. We have thus direct evidence that it was inserted into the former poem at a comparatively late period of its literary development. Of still greater interest is the date of the writing of the tablet, for it proves conclusively that an early date must be assigned to the legends which are known to us from tablets written in the seventh century for the library of Ashur-bāni-pal. In this fragmentary version of the deluge story, found upon a

[1] See Scheil, *Recueil de Travaux*, Vol. XX. (1898), pp. 55 ff.

tablet which was written more than 1300 years before Ashur-bāni-pal's time, the internal evidence furnished by the late Assyrian tablets is amply corroborated.

Returning to the account of the deluge preserved in the Gilgamesh poem, we there find a form of the legend which in general resembles the story reproduced from Berosus. We there read that the gods in the city of Shurippak decided to send a deluge upon the earth. In a dream the god Ea revealed their intention to a man of the city named Tsīt-napishtim who, in accordance with Ea's instructions, saved himself, and his family, and every kind of beast, by building a ship in which they escaped from the flood. The thread of the narrative is identical with that of Berosus, though it differs from it in details. The hero of the story, for instance, dwells in Shurippak, not in Sippar, and the god does not bid him write a history of the world to instruct posterity after the deluge has destroyed all other records. The warning of Xisuthros by Chronos, however, corresponds to that of Tsīt-napishtim by Ea, and the name Xisuthros finds its equivalent in Atrakhāsis, or Khāsisatra, a name by which Tsīt-napishtim is referred to in the speech of Ea at the end of the story. Both heroes, moreover, are deified after coming forth from the ship. With regard to the name Tsīt-napishtim, it must be mentioned that the reading of the first part of the name is still a matter of conjecture, and that some scholars render it Par-napishtim; whichever be correct the meaning of the name appears to be "the "offspring of life." It has already been stated that Ea refers to Tsīt-napishtim by the name Atrakhāsis, which means "abounding in wisdom"; and a theory has recently been put forward to account for the occurrence of these two names for the hero of the legend. According to it [1] the story of the deluge in the Gilgamesh epic is made up of two legends which have been interwoven. One was a nature myth describing a universal deluge, and the other a local legend referring to the destruction of a single city. Atrakhāsis is the hero of the nature myth, and Tsīt-napishtim, "the man of Shurippak," is the hero of the local legend; while both names are given to the hero in the story, as told in the poem of Gilgamesh. The theory is ingenious, but it lacks evidence.

Before proceeding to compare the Babylonian story of the flood with that preserved in Genesis, we give a translation of the former version, so far as the present state of preservation of the text will allow.[2] The whole story is put into the mouth of Tsīt-napishtim, who tells it to Gilgamesh, without interruption, from beginning to end. He begins by describing how the gods in council, in the city of Shurippak, decided to send a deluge upon the earth, and how Ea revealed the secret

---

[1] See Jastrow, *Zeitschrift für Assyriologie*, Bd. XIII. (1899), pp. 288 ff.

[2] Cf. Jeremias, *Izdubar-Nimrod*, pp. 32 ff.; Jensen, *Die Kosmologie der Babylonier*, pp. 367 ff.; and Zimmern in Gunkel's *Schöpfung und Chaos*, pp. 423 ff.

to Tsīt-napishtim, one of the dwellers in the town. The opening lines of Ea's address to Tsīt-napishtim, which begins, "O reed-hut, reed-hut! O wall, wall! "O reed-hut, hear! O wall, understand!" has proved a rather puzzling passage to commentators, for it is not quite obvious why Ea should address a dwelling in this manner when he gives his warning to Tsīt-napishtim. The best explanation of the passage seems to be that Ea, before speaking to Tsīt-napishtim, first addresses the hut in which he is sleeping. We know from the end of the story that Ea revealed the secret to Tsīt-napishtim in a vision, and, in view of the passage in Ea's speech, it is not unnatural to suppose that Tsīt-napishtim was sleeping at the time in a hut built of reeds, a common form of dwelling among the poorer inhabitants of Babylonia.

Tsīt-napishtim begins his story thus:—

"I will reveal to thee, O Gilgamesh, the hidden word,
"And the decision of the gods will I declare to thee.
"Shurippak, a city which thou knowest,
"Which lieth on the bank of the Euphrates,
"That city was old; and the gods within it,
"Their hearts prompted the great gods to send a deluge.[1]
"There was their father Anu,
"And their counsellor the warrior Bēl,

---

[1] *I.e.*, upon the city and mankind.

"And their messenger Ninib,
"And their governor Ennugi.
"The lord of wisdom, Ea, sat also with them,
"And he repeated their purpose to the hut of reeds, (saying):
"'O reed-hut, reed-hut! O wall, wall!
"O reed-hut, hear! O wall, understand!
"Thou man of Shurippak,[1] son of Ubara-Tutu,
"Pull down thy house, build a ship,
"Forsake thy possessions, take heed for thy life!
"Abandon thy goods, save thy life,
"And bring up living seed of every kind into the ship.
"As for the ship, which thou shalt build,
"Well planned must be its dimensions,
"Its breadth and its length shall bear proportion each to each,
"And thou shalt launch it in the ocean!'
"I took heed, and spake unto Ea, my lord, (saying):
"'[The command], O my lord, which thou hast given,
"I will honour, and will fulfil.
"But how shall I make answer unto the city, the people and the elders thereof?'
"Ea opened his mouth and spake,
"And he said unto me, his servant,
"'Thus shalt thou answer and say unto them:
"Bēl hath cast me forth, for he hateth me,

[1] *I.e.*, Tsīt-napishtim.

"And I can no longer live in your city;
"Nor on Bēl's earth can I any longer lay my head.
"I will therefore go down to the deep and dwell with
my lord Ea.'"

The next few lines, which contain the end of the answer which Tsīt-napishtim is to give to the people, are broken, and their meaning is not quite plain. The general drift of the passage seems to be that his departure will bring blessings on the land he is leaving, for Bēl will shower down upon it multitudes of birds and fish, and will grant a plenteous harvest. They will know when to expect their prosperity, for Shamash has set an appointed time, when the lord of darkness, the god Rammān, will pour down upon them an abundant rain. According to this interpretation Tsīt-napishtim is ordered to allay any misgivings that his fellow citizens may feel by assuring them beforehand that the signs of the deluge are marks of coming prosperity, and not of destruction. Some explain the passage by assuming that Tsīt-napishtim is to make no secret of the coming deluge, but to foretell its advent and the destruction of all living things including birds and fish. The former rendering seems to agree better with the earlier part of his answer; otherwise Ea would have told him to say that Bēl hated, not himself only, but mankind at large.

Quite a different version of Ea's instructions to Tsīt-napishtim and of his answer to the god is given

THE BUILDING OF THE SHIP. 131

on another tablet, of which only a fragment has been recovered. According to this version Ea told him to watch for the appointed time and then to enter the ship, wherein he was to bring his corn, and his property, and his possessions, and his family, and his household and handicraftsmen, together with certain cattle and beasts of the field. In his answer to the god Tsīt-napishtim does not ask how he is to explain his action to his fellow citizens, and only seems to be troubled by the practical difficulties of his task. He complains that he has never yet built a ship, and

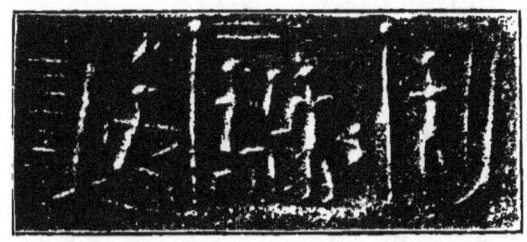

A Babylonian ship. (From a cylinder-seal in the British Museum, No. 89,349.)

therefore asks the god to trace out a plan of the vessel upon the ground. At this point the version breaks off.

After receiving Ea's commands Tsīt-napishtim collected the wood and the materials necessary for the construction of the ship for four whole days, and on the fifth day he laid it down. He made the hull in the form of a flat-bottomed barge, 120 cubits in width. Upon the hull he constructed a sort of house or cabin, 120 cubits in height. This great deck-house he divided into six stories, and each story contained nine rooms. The outside of the ship he rendered watertight by pouring six measures of bitumen over it, and the inside he smeared with pitch. He then caused oil to be brought and he slaughtered oxen; and, after filling jars with sesame-wine, and oil, and grape-wine, he held a feast "like that of New Year's "Day." On the seventh day the ship was ready, and Tsit-napishtim then hastened to carry out Ea's instructions, and to fill it with all that he possessed. The narrative continues :—

"With all that I had I filled it.

"With all the silver I had, I filled it,

"With all the gold I had, I filled it,

"With all living seed of every kind that I possessed, I filled it.

"I brought up into the ship all my family and household,

"The cattle of the field, and the beasts of the field, the handicraftsmen—all of them I brought in.

"A fixed time Shamash had appointed, (saying):

"'The lord of darkness will at eventide send a heavy rain;

"Then go into the ship, and shut thy door.'

"The appointed season arrived, and

"The ruler of the darkness sent at eventide a heavy rain.

"Of the storm I saw the beginning;

THE COMING OF THE FLOOD.

" To look upon the storm I was afraid;
" I entered into the ship and shut the door.
" To the pilot of the ship, to Puzur-Bêl the sailor,
" I committed the great building,[1] and the contents thereof.
" When the early dawn appeared,
" There came up from the horizon a black cloud.
" Rammān in the midst thereof thundered,
" And Nabū and Marduk went before,
" They passed like messengers over mountain and country.
" Uragal parted the anchor-cable.
" There went Ninib, and he made the storm to burst.
" The Anunnaki carried flaming torches,
" And with the brightness thereof they lit up the earth.
" The whirlwind of Rammān mounted up into the heavens, and
" All light was turned into darkness."

The tempest raged for a whole day. The waters rose, and all was confusion; men by reason of the darkness could see nothing, and they perished miserably. The text continues:—

" No man beheld his fellow,
" No longer could men know each other. In heaven

[1] *I.e.*, the ship.

"The gods were afraid of the deluge,
"They retreated, they went up into the heaven of Anu.
"The gods crouched down like hounds,
"In the enclosure (of heaven) they sat cowering.
"Then Ishtar cried aloud like a woman in travail,
"The Lady of the gods lamented with a loud voice, (saying):
"'The old race of man hath been turned back into clay,
"Because I assented to an evil thing in the council of the gods!
"Alas! I have assented to an evil thing in the council of the gods,
"And agreed to a storm which hath destroyed my people!
"That which I brought forth—where is it?
"Like the spawn of fish it filleth the sea!'
"The gods of the Anunnaki wept with her,
"The gods were bowed down, they sat down weeping,
"Their lips were pressed together . . .
"For six days and six nights
"The wind blew, and the deluge and the tempest overwhelmed the land.
"When the seventh day drew nigh, then ceased the tempest and the deluge, and the storm,
"Which had fought like a host.
"Then the sea became quiet and it went down; and the hurricane and the deluge ceased.

"I looked upon the sea and cried aloud,
"For all mankind was turned back into clay.
"In place of the fields a swamp lay before me.
"I opened the window and the light fell upon my cheek;
"I bowed myself down, I sat down, I wept;
"Over my cheek flowed my tears.
"I looked upon the world, and behold all was sea.
"After twelve (days?) the land appeared,
"To the land Nitsir the ship took its course.
"The mountain of the land of Nitsir held the ship fast and did not let it slip.
"The first day, the second day, the mountain Nitsir held the ship fast.
"The third day, the fourth day, the mountain Nitsir held the ship fast.
"The fifth day, the sixth day, the mountain Nitsir held the ship fast.
"When the seventh day drew nigh, I sent out a dove, and let her go forth.
"The dove flew hither and thither,
"But there was no resting-place (for her) and she returned.
"Then I sent out a swallow, and let her go forth.
"The swallow flew hither and thither,
"But there was no resting-place (for her) and she returned.
"Then I sent out a raven and let her go forth.

"The raven flew away and beheld the abatement of the waters,
"And she came near, wading and croaking, but did not return.
"Then I brought (all) out unto the four winds, I offered an offering,
"I made a libation on the peak of the mountain.
"By sevens I set out the vessels,
"Under them I heaped up reed, and cedar-wood, and incense.
"The gods smelt the savour,
"The gods smelt the sweet savour,
"The gods gathered like flies about him that offered up the sacrifice.
"Then the Lady of the gods drew nigh,
"And she lifted up the great jewels, which Anu had made according to her wish, (and said):
"'What gods these are! By the jewels of *lapis lazuli* which are upon my neck, I will not forget!
"These days I have set in my memory, never will I forget them!
"Let the gods come to the offering,
"But Bêl shall not come to the offering,
"Since he refused to ask counsel and sent the deluge,
"And handed over my people unto destruction.'
"Now when Bêl drew nigh,
"He saw the ship, and he was very wroth;

EA'S PROTEST.

"He was filled with anger against the gods, the Igigi, (saying):
"'Who then hath escaped with his life?
"No man shall live after the destruction!'
"Then Ninib opened his mouth and spake,
"And said to the warrior Bêl,
"'Who but Ea could have done this thing?
"For Ea knoweth every matter!'
"Then Ea opened his mouth and spake,
"And said to the warrior Bêl,
"'Thou art the governor of the gods, O warrior,
"But thou wouldst not take counsel and thou hast sent the deluge!
"On the sinner visit his sin, and
"On the transgressor visit his transgression;
"But hold thy hand, that all be not destroyed!
"And forbear (?), that all be not [confounded]!
"Instead of sending a deluge,
"Let a lion come and minish mankind!
"Instead of sending a deluge,
"Let a leopard come and minish mankind!
"Instead of sending a deluge,
"Let a famine come and [waste] the land!
"Instead of sending a deluge,
"Let the Plague-god come and [slay] mankind!
"I did not reveal the purpose of the great gods.
"I caused Atrakhāsis to see a dream, and (thus) he heard the purpose of the gods.'

"Thereupon Bēl arrived at a decision,
"And he went up into the ship.
"He took my hand and brought me forth,
"He brought my wife forth, he made her to kneel at my side,
"He turned towards us, he stood between us, he blessed us, (saying) :
"'Hitherto hath Tsīt-napishtim been of mankind,
"But now let Tsīt-napishtim be like unto the gods, even us,
"And let Tsīt-napishtim dwell afar off at the mouth of the river!'
"Then they took me, and afar off, at the mouth of the rivers, they made me to dwell."

The reader will now have gained a notion of the form of the deluge story current in Assyria during the seventh century B.C., but, before comparing it with the Biblical account, it will be necessary to consider the following facts. The Biblical story is contained in Gen. vi. 9—ix. 17, and, like the stories of the creation given in the first and second chapters of that book, is taken from two separate writings—the "Priestly "writing" and the "Jehovist narrative," brief descriptions of which have already been given.[1] In the case of the accounts of the creation we have seen that the two stories were not interwoven one with the other, and that one was first given and then the other. In

---

[1] See above, pp. 110 f.

the case of the deluge on the other hand, the two accounts are not given separately, but have been united so as to form a single narrative. The compiler, however, has made very little alteration in his two sources of information, and has scrupulously preserved the texts upon which he has drawn. Even where the two versions differ from each other in points of detail he has not attempted to harmonize them, but without change has given each as he found it; thanks to this fact it is possible to disentangle the two accounts with absolute certainty.

As the text reads at present we find considerable differences in certain passages with regard to two important details of the story, *viz.*, the length of the duration of the deluge, and the number of the animals which were preserved. According to Gen. vii. 10, the flood took place seven days after Noah was told to build the ark; in Gen. vii. 12 and viii. 6, the waters are said to have prevailed for forty days; and according to Gen. viii. 6-12, the waters subsided after three periods of seven days each. These passages give the total duration of the deluge, including the seven days of preparation, as sixty-eight days. On the other hand, in Gen. vii. 11, the flood is said to have begun "in the six hundredth year of Noah's life, in the "second month, on the seventeenth day of the month"; in Gen. vii. 24, it is stated that "the waters prevailed "upon the earth an hundred and fifty days"; and according to Gen. viii. 13 and 14, the waters finally disappeared, and the earth became dry in the "six "hundred and first year" of Noah, "in the second "month, on the seven and twentieth day of the "month." Thus, according to these passages, the total duration of the deluge was more than a year —a statement that is not compatible with the previously cited passages which give the length of its duration as sixty-eight days. The second most striking instance of divergence occurs in the numbers of the animals to be preserved in the ark; according to Gen. vi. 19, Noah is told to preserve two of every sort, while in Gen. vii. 2, Noah is to preserve seven of every clean beast, and two of every beast that is not clean. These are perhaps the two most striking instances of divergence in the narrative, for they cannot be reconciled except on the supposition that they are the accounts of two different writers which have been interwoven with each other.

Other evidence, such as the occurrence of double accounts of the same episode, each written in a style of its own, points in the same direction; and it is possible on the basis of such evidence to separate the two threads of the narrative. These two threads are so distinct that any one may trace them for himself in the Authorized Version of the English Bible. This will be apparent if we mark with a line at the side of the column the following passages of the narrative: Gen. vi. 9-22; vii. 6, 11, 13-16 (down to "as God commanded him"); vii. 18-21 and 24; viii. 1 and 2 (down to "were stopped"); viii. 3 (from "and after the end") -5; viii. 13 (down to "from off the earth"); viii. 14-19; and ix. 1-17. When this has been done and these passages read consecutively, it will be seen that we have a perfectly complete and consistent account of the deluge. If the passages which have been left unmarked are next read, it will be seen that, although one fragment of a verse has been transposed (chapter vii., the second half of verse 16), we have here another complete and consistent account of the deluge.[1]

[1] This will be apparent from the following summaries; we will summarize the marked passages first, which together contain the account of the deluge according to the "Priestly writing":—Because the earth was corrupt God decided to send a deluge. He therefore warned Noah to build an ark, giving him precise directions with regard to its size and to the mode of its construction; when it was finished he was told to bring his own family into the ark, and two of every kind of living creature, male and female, as well as food for himself and for them; Noah did as he was commanded (vi. 9-22). Noah was six hundred years old when the flood began (vii. 6); in the six hundredth year of his life the flood was caused by the breaking up of the fountains of the great deep and by the opening of the windows of heaven (vii. 11). On the self-same day Noah and his family entered the ark, and he brought in the animals in pairs (vii. 13-16). And the waters increased and covered the high mountains, and the depth of the flood was fifteen cubits, and every living creature perished (vii. 18-21). And the waters prevailed for an hundred and fifty days, when God sent a wind to assuage the waters; and the fountains of the deep and the windows of heaven were stopped (vii. 24-viii. 2). After the end of the hundred and fifty days the waters decreased and in the seventh month the ark rested upon the mountains of Ararat. And the waters decreased continually until the tenth month, when

SUMMARY OF THE ACCOUNTS.

The reader will see that each account repeats phrases characteristic to itself, and each, when separated from the other, contains a consistent and uncontradictory

the tops of the mountains were seen (viii. 3-5). And on the first day of the six hundred and first year the waters were dried up from the earth (viii. 13), and by the seven and twentieth day of the second month the earth was quite dry (viii. 14). And Noah came forth from the ark (viii. 15-19), and God blessed Noah and his sons, and He made a covenant that He would not again send a flood to destroy the earth, and as a token of the covenant He set His rainbow in the clouds (ix. 1-17). Such is the story, complete and consistent with itself, which is given by the marked passages.

The unmarked passages represent the "Jehovistic narrative." In the marked passages the reader will have noticed that the Divine name used is "God," which corresponds to the Hebrew word "Elō-"hīm"; in the unmarked passages he will notice that the word generally used is "the Lord," representing the Hebrew word "Jahveh" or Jehovah. The "Jehovistic narrative" is not quite a complete account, for its beginning, which contained the command to build the ark, is omitted, doubtless because the "Priestly writing" gives so full an account of it. From what remains of the "Jehovistic "narrative" we gain the following picture of the flood:—Since Noah had been righteous in his generation, the Lord bade him and all his house go up into the ark. Noah was also told to bring into the ark with him seven of every kind of clean beast and two of every unclean beast, the greater number of clean beasts no doubt being taken to serve as food during the time Noah and his household should be shut up in the ark. Noah was warned that in seven days' time the Lord would cause it to rain upon the earth for forty days and forty nights, and every living thing the Lord had made would be destroyed (vii. 1-5). Noah therefore did as he was commanded; he took the clean and unclean beasts into the ark with him (vii. 7-9) and the Lord shut him in (vii. 16). As had been foretold, after seven days the flood came upon the earth (vii. 10),.and the rain was upon the earth forty days and forty nights (vii. 12). And the flood was forty days upon the earth, and the waters increased and bore up the ark (vii. 17); and every living thing was destroyed, except Noah and they that were with him in the ark (vii. 22 and 23). Then the rain from heaven was restrained and the waters returned from off the earth continually (viii. 2 and 3), and at the end of forty days Noah opened the window narrative of the event. The "Priestly writing," in accordance with its annalistic character, gives exact details concerning the size and structure of the ark, records the depth of the flood in cubits, gives precise dates, by day and month and year, as to when the flood began, when the ark rested upon Ararat, when the tops of the mountains were seen, when the waters were dried up, and also when the earth was quite dry. Episodes peculiar to it are the breaking up of the fountains of the deep as a cause of the flood, the resting of the ark on the mountains of Ararat, and the making of the covenant with the rainbow as its token. The "Jehovistic narrative" is far more picturesque; the Lord shuts Noah into the ark, He smells the sweet savour of Noah's sacrifice, and He says in His heart He will not again send a deluge. The episodes peculiar to this account are the distinction made between clean and unclean animals, the bringing

of the ark and sent forth a raven, which flew to and fro and did not return; then a dove, which, finding no rest for the sole of her foot, returned to him. He waited another seven days and again he sent forth the dove, which this time brought in her mouth an olive leaf plucked off; so Noah knew the waters were abated. He waited yet another seven days and then again sent forth the dove, which this time did not return (viii. 6-12). So Noah removed the covering of the ark and beheld that the face of the ground was dried (viii. 13). And Noah built an altar unto the Lord, and took of every clean beast and of every clean fowl and offered burnt offerings on the altar. And the Lord smelled the sweet savour, and said in His heart He would not again curse the ground nor smite every living thing; while the earth remained, the natural order of the universe should not be changed (viii. 20-22).

on of the deluge by a heavy rain only and not by the breaking up of the fountains of the great deep, the sending forth of the raven and the dove, the building of the altar and the sacrifice to Jehovah. The chief points of divergence between the two narratives, that is to say, the statements as to the length of the flood's duration, have been referred to already.

When we compare the Babylonian account of the deluge with these two versions in the book of Genesis, we see that it contains many of the peculiarities of both. The details with regard to the form and structure of the ship are very similar to those of the ark in the "Priestly writing," both accounts stating that the vessel was built in stories, and that pitch was used for making it watertight; in both narratives the ark is said to have rested upon a mountain; and Ea's protest against the sending of a deluge in the future is perhaps the equivalent of God's covenant with Noah that mankind should not again be so destroyed. On the other hand, many of the features peculiar to the "Jehovistic narrative" also appear in the Babylonian version. Such are the seven days which elapsed between the warning and the coming of the deluge, the cause of the deluge ascribed to heavy rain, the sending forth of birds to test the condition of the waters, the burning of a sacrifice from which a sweet savour rose, etc.

ORIGIN OF THE HEBREW VERSIONS. 145

We have therefore in Genesis beyond doubt two independent versions of the deluge story, both originally derived from Babylonian sources, but neither directly copied from the Babylonian version as we know it on the tablets from Ashur-bāni-pal's library. In the case of the legends of the creation we have already noted indications that they were derived from Babylon at some period prior to the exile, and the arguments there brought forward apply with equal force to the story of the deluge. It is a striking fact, however, that the latter narrative has not left so strong a mark upon the earlier Hebrew writings as did the Babylonian dragon-myth. In the second half of the book of Isaiah the wrath of Jehovah in sending the Jews into captivity is compared to "the waters of Noah,"[1] and in Ezekiel[2] also there is an interesting reference to Noah, which presupposes a knowledge of the Biblical story of the flood; but traces of the story in the other books of the Old Testament are not very numerous. Moreover the resemblance between the Hebrew and the Babylonian versions of the deluge is very much closer than that between the corresponding accounts of the creation. These facts indicate a later date for the adoption of the deluge story by the Hebrews, but a date which may have been centuries before the taking of Jerusalem.

[1] Isaiah liv. 9.   [2] Ezekiel xiv. 12-20.

CHAPTER V.

TALES OF GODS AND HEROES.

In the two preceding chapters we have described the legends of the Babylonians which have left their mark upon Hebrew literature. Of such legends those which dealt with the creation of the world formed in themselves a complete body of traditions, and these we have treated as such in Chapter III. The story of the deluge, on the other hand, which formed the subject of Chapter IV., has not come down to us as a separate legend, but occurs in the course of a long poem which describes the adventures of a great Babylonian hero named Gilgamesh. As the account of the deluge there narrated forms a complete story, we took it from its context, in order to treat it in connection with the legends of creation. We will now describe the remaining portions of this great poem of the Babylonians, which deals with the exploits of Gilgamesh, the greatest mythical hero of their race.

The name of the hero was, for many years, read "Izdubar," or "Gishdubar," but we now know that the

Babylonians pronounced the ideogram which formed the name, "Gilgamesh."[1] It has been suggested that Gilgamesh is to be identified with the hero Nimrod, who was "a mighty hunter before the Lord," and the beginning of whose kingdom was "Babel, and "Erech, and Accad, and Calneh, in the land of "Shinar";[2] but, beyond the fact that both Nimrod and Gilgamesh were great Babylonian heroes of antiquity, there are no other grounds for assuming their identity. Of Nimrod we know little besides what is told us in the passage in Genesis referred to, but the deeds of Gilgamesh are recounted in the longest Babylonian poem that has come down to us. It is written upon a series of twelve tablets, which, like those of the Creation series, are distinguished by numbers. The late Sir Henry C. Rawlinson made the suggestion that the poem was a solar myth, the twelve tablets corresponding to the twelve months of the year, but the contents of the majority of the tablets do not fit in with this view of their origin. In fact, it is probable that the division of the poem into twelve sections was a comparatively late arrangement, the work of the scribes who collected and edited the ancient legends. We know that stories and legends of the hero Gilgamesh go back into

---

[1] Ælian mentions an ancient king Gilgamos, a name he evidently took from the hero of this poem.
[2] Gen. x. 8-10.

remote antiquity, for cylinder-seals, made during the Sumerian period,[1] have been found, on which are engraved the deeds of valour performed by him. The actual poem, however, in which we read these stories, like most of the other legends of the Babylonians, is known to us from Assyrian tablets which were written in the seventh century before Christ. Several copies of the work were made for Ashur-bāni-pal's library, and, from the numerous fragments of them that are in the British Museum, it is possible to piece together the story, and to give several of the episodes of the narrative in detail.[2] The story clings to the ancient city of Erech, the chief seat of the worship of the goddess Ishtar, and, although in the course of his adventures, Gilgamesh travelled into distant lands, he always returned to the city of Erech.

The First Tablet of the series is much broken. A fragment has been found which not improbably contained the opening words of the poem, for it seems to describe the benefits that will accrue to a man who will study the poem and make himself acquainted with the hero's history. After these prefatory remarks, the text introduces the name of Erech, and describes the misfortunes that have fallen upon this ancient city in consequence of a siege that has taken place. All living things that are in the city, gods, and men,

---

[1] *I.e.*, from about B.C. 4000 to B.C. 2300.
[2] Cf. Jeremias, *Izdubar-Nimrod*, Leipzig, 1891.

and beasts, are confused and terrified; the text reads as follows:—

"She asses [tread down] their young,
"Cows [turn upon] their calves.
"Men cry aloud like beasts,
"And maidens mourn like doves.
"The gods of strong-walled Erech
"Are changed to flies, and buzz about the streets.
"The spirits of strong-walled Erech
"Are changed to serpents, and glide into holes (?).
"For three years the enemy besieged Erech,
"And the doors were barred, and the bolts were shot,
"And Ishtar did not raise her head against the foe."

We have no mention of Gilgamesh upon these fragments of the First Tablet, but, as on the Second Tablet we find the inhabitants of Erech groaning under his rule, it is not improbable that the foe mentioned as besieging Erech was led by Gilgamesh, and that they succeeded in capturing the city. Another view is that Gilgamesh came forward and delivered Erech from her enemies, and in return for his services was elected ruler of the city. By whichever of these means he obtained his throne in Erech, there is no doubt that his rule soon became unpopular, for he forced all the young men of the city into his service and carried off the maidens to his court. The elders complained, saying:—

"Gilgamesh hath not left the son to his father,
"Nor the maid to the hero, nor the wife to her
    husband."

They therefore cried to the goddess Aruru against the tyranny of Gilgamesh, complaining that he acted in this despotic manner because he had no rival to keep him in check. Day and night the people raised their complaint, and the gods of heaven heard them and had compassion upon them. And the gods also cried aloud to Aruru, bidding her create a being, equal to Gilgamesh in strength, who might fight with him and limit his power. They urged that as she had created Gilgamesh,[1] so she must now create his rival. Aruru listened to their words and proceeded to plan and to create a being who should be capable of opposing Gilgamesh. The passage referring to the creation of this being, who was named Ea-bani, reads as follows:—

"Upon hearing these words (*i.e.*, the words of the gods)
"Aruru conceived a man of Anu[2] in her mind.
"Aruru washed her hands,
"She broke off a piece of clay, she cast it on the
    ground.
"Thus she created Ea-bani, the hero."

Ea-bani, however, was not wholly human in form.

---

[1] It will be remembered that according to one version of the Creation story, the goddess Aruru, in company with Marduk, is credited with the creation of mankind; see above, p. 90.

[2] *I.e.*, a divine man, a demi-god. In this phrase "Anu" is used as a general name for "god."

THE CREATION OF EA-BANI.

From his picture upon cylinder-seals we know that he had the head, and body, and arms of a man, but his legs were those of a beast. The following description of Ea-bani is given in the poem:—

"The whole of his body was [covered] with hair,
"He was clothed with long hair like a woman.
"The quality of his hair was luxuriant, like that of the Corn-god.
"He knew [not] the land and the inhabitants thereof,
"He was clothed with garments as the god of the field.
"With the gazelles he ate herbs,
"With the beasts he slaked his thirst,
"With the creatures of the water his heart rejoiced."

A new personage now comes on the scene and, from the abruptness with which he is introduced, it is evident that he has already been described in some previous portion of the poem that is wanting. This new personage is Tsâidu, "the hunter," who appears to have been sent into the mountains by Gilgamesh in order to capture Ea-bani. The gods no doubt in due time would have brought Ea-bani to Erech to do battle with Gilgamesh, and the object of Gilgamesh in sending Tsâidu to capture Ea-bani was clearly to forestall their intention. "The hunter" accordingly went out into the mountains and lay in wait for Ea-bani. For three days Tsâidu watched Ea-bani as he went down to the stream to drink, but he thought he was too strong to overcome in single combat. He therefore returned to Erech and told Gilgamesh of the monster's strength; he described his own terror at beholding him, and added that he destroyed all the traps which had been set for him, saying:—

" He rangeth over [all] the mountains,
" Regularly with the beasts [he feedeth],
" Regularly his feet [are set] towards the drinking-place.
" But I was afraid, I could not approach him.
" He hath filled up the pit which I digged,
" He hath destroyed the nets which I [spread],
" He hath caused the cattle and the beasts of the field to escape from my hands,
" And he doth not let me make war (upon them)."

Gilgamesh was not discouraged by Tsāidu's want of success, and he revealed to him a device by which he might capture Ea-bani, who had proved too cunning for the ordinary snares of the hunter, saying:—

" Go, my Tsāidu, and take Ukhat with thee.
" And when the beasts come down to the drinking-place,
" Then let her tear off her clothing and disclose her nakedness.
" (Ea-bani) shall see her, and he shall draw nigh unto her,
" And the cattle, which grew up on his field, shall forsake him."

Ukhat, whom Tsāidu was told to take with him, was one of the sacred women who were in the service of Ishtar and were attached to the ancient temple of that goddess in the city of Erech. The narrative continues:—

"Tsāidu departed, and took with him the woman Ukhat.
"They took the straight road,
"And on the third day they reached the appointed place.
"Then Tsāidu and the woman placed themselves in hiding.
"For one day, for two days, they lurked by the drinking-place.
"With the beasts (Ea-bani) slaked his thirst,
"With the creatures of the waters his heart rejoiced.
"Then Ea-bani (approached) . . . ,
"With the gazelles he ate herbs,
"With the beasts he slaked his thirst,
"With the creatures of the water his heart rejoiced."

As Ea-bani came near, Ukhat caught sight of him, and Tsāidu exclaimed:—

"That is he, Ukhat, loosen thy girdle,
"Uncover thy nakedness that he may receive thy favours,
"Be not faint-hearted, lay hold upon his soul.
"He shall see thee, and shall draw nigh unto thee.
"Open thy garment, and he shall lie in thine arms.

"Give him pleasure after the manner of women.
"His cattle, which grew up in his field, shall forsake him,
"While he holdeth thee in the embraces of love."

Ukhat did as Tsāidu bade her, and the plot was attended with success, as we may see from the following lines :—

"Ukhat loosened her garment, she uncovered her nakedness,
"She was not faint-hearted, and she laid hold upon his soul.
"She opened her garment, and he lay in her arms.
"She gave him pleasure after the manner of women,
"And he held her in the embraces of love.
"For six days and six nights Ea-bani drew nigh and tarried with Ukhat.
"After he had satisfied himself with her abundance,
"He turned his attention to his cattle.
"His gazelles lay, and looked at Ea-bani,
"The beasts of the field turned away from him.
"Ea-bani was terrified, his body grew stiff,
"His knees stood still, as his cattle departed."

Ea-bani, however, did not attempt to pursue them or to induce them to return to him. Recovering from his dismay he turned once more to the companion at his side and—

"He returned to love, he sat at the feet of the woman,

" And he gazed up into her face,
" And as the woman spake he listened.
" And the woman said unto Ea-bani:
" ' Thou art of great stature, O Ea-bani, and art like
    unto a god.
" Why then dost thou lie with the beasts of the field ?
" Come, let me bring thee to strong-walled Erech,
" To the bright house, the dwelling of Anu and
    Ishtar,
" To the palace of Gilgamesh, who is perfect in
    strength,
" And who, like a mountain-bull, wieldeth power
    over men.'
" She spake unto him and he hearkened unto her
    word,
" In the wisdom of his heart he wished for a friend.
" Ea-bani spake unto the woman :
" ' Come then, Ukhat, lead me away,
" To the bright and holy dwelling of Anu and Ishtar,
" To the palace of Gilgamesh, who is perfect in
    strength,
" And who like [a mountain-bull wieldeth power]
    over men.' "

The text of the poem which follows is broken, and it is only with difficulty that the thread of the narrative can be made out. Ea-bani had heard so much of the might of Gilgamesh from Ukhat that he desired to win his friendship ; but, it appears, he first wished to test the hero's strength, and to join with him in battle. It was with this object that he set out with Ukhat for the city of Erech, and they happened to arrive there during the celebration of a festival. Ea-bani, however, had a dream in which he was warned to refrain from attempting to do battle with Gilgamesh. He was told that Gilgamesh was more powerful than he, and that, as by day and by night he did not rest, he could not hope to take him unawares. He was also told in his dream that Gilgamesh was beloved of Shamash, the Sun-god, and that the three great gods, Anu, Bêl, and Ea, had given wisdom unto him.

Meanwhile Gilgamesh also had a dream, and he was troubled because he could not interpret it. He therefore went to his mother Aruru and enquired of her the meaning of his vision. He told her that in his vision the stars of heaven seemed to fall upon him, and his mother seems to have interpreted the dream as foretelling the coming of Ea-bani, and also to have advised him to make friends with Ea-bani.

Gilgamesh and Ea-bani did not enter into combat, and the Third Tablet of the series tells how they became friends. From the fragments of the text which remain, it appears that Ea-bani did not at first give heed to the warning vouchsafed him in his dream, and it was only after the personal intervention of the Sun-god that he gave up the desire to do battle with Gilgamesh, and consented to treat him henceforth as his comrade. In order to induce Ea-bani to remain at Erech, Shamash conferred on him royal rank, and he promised him that he should recline on a great couch while the princes of the earth kissed his feet, and that the people of Erech should proclaim their submission unto him. Ea-bani listened to the Sun-god, and consented to remain in Erech as the friend of Gilgamesh.

The next section of the poem is also incomplete, but enough of the text remains to enable us to make out the story, which concerns an expedition undertaken by both heroes against an Elamite despot[1] named Khumbaba. The preparations for the expedition and the battle with Khumbaba are described upon the Fourth and Fifth Tablets of the series. Before setting out for the castle of Khumbaba, Ea-bani prayed to the Sun-god, and Gilgamesh recounted to his friend a favourable dream which had been sent to him, in which he beheld the dead body of Khumbaba. In due time the two heroes came to a wood of cedar trees, in the middle of which Khumbaba's castle was built. Khumbaba was feared by all who dwelt near him, for his roaring was like the storm, and any man, who was rash enough to enter into his cedar wood, perished. The two heroes, however, undismayed by the reports of their enemy's power, pressed forward

[1] The people of Elam, which was situated to the east of Mesopotamia, were, from an early period, in constant conflict with Babylonia.

on their journey. They entered the wood, but were amazed at the great size of the trees that grew therein, and in the words of the poem—

"They stood still, and marvelled at the wood,
"They gazed at the height of the cedars,
"They gazed at the entrance of the wood,
"The place where Khumbaba was wont to walk and set his foot.
"The road had been laid out, and the path was well made."

After describing the beauty of the greatest of the cedars, which possessed a pleasant and delightful shade and a sweet smell, the tablet breaks off. How the heroes penetrated to the castle, and in what manner they succeeded in slaying Khumbaba, we do not know; but that they were successful in the fight is clear from the last line of the tablet. Half this line is preserved and reads "the head of Khumbaba," from which we may perhaps infer that Gilgamesh and Ea-bani, after slaying the tyrant, cut off his head from his body.

Hitherto the heroes had only met with success. Enjoying the favour of the Sun-god, they had succeeded in slaying a powerful enemy of their city, and they now returned to Erech elated with their victory. From this time forward, however, their lot was not so happy, and the Sixth Tablet gives the reason of their misfortunes, for it narrates how Gilgamesh incurred the wrath of the powerful goddess Ishtar. The tablet opens with an account of how, on his return from Erech, Gilgamesh removed the stains of battle, and clothed himself in his royal robes, in the following words:—

"[He cleansed] his weapons, he polished his weapons,
"[He removed] his armour from upon him,
"[He took off] his soiled garments, he clothed himself in clean raiment.
"He donned [his robes of] honour, he bound on his diadem,
"Gilgamesh wore his crown, he bound on his diadem."

The sight of the hero thus arrayed on his return from battle kindled with love for him the heart of the goddess Ishtar. The poem tells how she beheld the comeliness of Gilgamesh, and addressed him in these words:—

"Come, Gilgamesh, be thou my spouse.
"Bestow thy strength upon me as a gift,
"And thou shalt be my husband, and I will be thy wife.
"I will set thee in a chariot of *lapis lazuli* and gold,
"With wheels made of gold and horns made of diamonds,
"And mighty . . . steeds shalt thou yoke to it.
"Thou shalt enter our house with the sweet scent of cedars.
"When thou enterest our house,

"[The great and] the mighty shall kiss thy feet.
"Kings, and rulers, and princes shall bow down before thee,
"And from mountain and plain shall they bring gifts unto thee as tribute."

The goddess promised in addition that his flocks should bear twins, that the horses of his chariot should be swift, and that his cattle should be unrivalled. But Gilgamesh refused her proffered love, remembering the fate of those who had already enjoyed it, and thus upbraided her with her treachery :—

"On Tammuz, the spouse of thy youth,
"Thou didst lay affliction every year.
"Thou didst love the brilliant Allalu-bird,
"But thou didst smite him and break his wing;
"He stands in the woods, and cries, 'O my wing.'
"Thou didst also love a lion, perfect in strength,
"Seven by seven didst thou dig snares for him.
"Thou didst also love a horse, pre-eminent in battle
"Bridle, spur, and whip didst thou lay upon him,
"Thou didst make him to gallop for seven *kasbu*,
"Trouble and sweating didst thou force him to bear,
"And on his mother Silili thou didst lay affliction.
"Thou didst also love a shepherd of the flock,
. "Who continually poured out for thee the libation (?),
"And daily slaughtered kids for thee;
"But thou didst smite him, and didst change him into a leopard,

"So that his own sheep-boy hunted him,
"And his own hounds tore him to pieces."

Gilgamesh also recounted the sad fate of a gardener in the service of Anu, Ishtar's father, whom she had loved. Every day he brought her costly gifts and made bright the dish from which she ate; but when she grew tired of him she changed him into a cripple, so that henceforth he could not rise from his bed. Gilgamesh ended his taunts with the words, "As for me, thou "wouldst love me, and like unto them thou wouldst "[afflict me]."

When Ishtar heard this she was enraged and she went up into heaven, where she sought out her father Anu, and her mother Anatu, and complained that Gilgamesh had scorned her. Anu attempted to soothe her, but she demanded vengeance upon Gilgamesh, and asked Anu to create a monstrous bull, named Alū, which should destroy the hero. Anu yielded to his imperious daughter and created the bull in accordance with her wish. The account of the battle between the bull and the two heroes Ea-bani and Gilgamesh, is very incomplete, but the struggle seems to have been long and fierce, and towards the end of the account we read that Ea-bani seized the bull by the tail so that Gilgamesh was no doubt enabled to slay the monster with his sword. In the accompanying illustration, we see Gilgamesh and Ea-bani each engaged in conflict with a bull. The picture may possibly be based upon some variant form of the legend, according to which Anu sent two divine bulls against Gilgamesh and his friend. Perhaps it is simpler, however, to regard it as a picture of the two heroes on a hunting expedition, for on other cylinder-seals they are frequently represented as struggling with several bulls and lions at the same time. It will be noticed that in the centre of the picture is a fir tree growing upon what appears to be a pile of stones.

Ea-bani and Gilgamesh in conflict with two bulls. (From a cylinder-seal in the British Museum, No. 89,308.)

The small half circles, however, which look like stones, are conventional representations of mountains; the engraver intended to convey the impression that the fight with the bulls took place in a well-wooded and mountainous country.

The poem next describes the wrath of Ishtar at the death of the bull as follows :—

"Then Ishtar went up on to the wall of strong-walled Erech;

"She mounted to the top and she uttered a curse, (saying),

"'Cursed be Gilgamesh, who has provoked me to anger,
"And has slain the bull from heaven.'
"When Ea-bani heard these words of Ishtar,
"He tore out the entrails (?) of the bull,
"And he cast them before her, (crying),
"'As for thee, I will conquer thee,
"And I will do to thee even as I have done to him.'"

Thus Ea-bani drew down upon himself the wrath of Ishtar.

Then Ishtar assembled the three grades of priestesses attached to her service and they made lamentation over the death of the bull.

The horns of the bull were of great value, for they were exceedingly large and each of them held six measures of oil. Gilgamesh, therefore, in gratitude for his victory, dedicated them to the Sun-god, who is described in this passage of the poem under the local name of Lugal-Marada, that is "King of Marad," Marad being a city in Babylonia. After dedicating the horns with much ceremony at the altar of the god, Gilgamesh and his attendants washed their hands in the Euphrates and then set out for Erech. On their arrival they rode through the streets of the city, and the people gathered together to gaze upon them as they passed. The princesses of the city also came out to meet Gilgamesh, and he cried out unto them, saying—

"Who is glorious among heroes?
"Who is mighty among men?
"Gilgamesh is glorious among heroes,
"Gilgamesh is mighty among men."

In this manner he passed through Erech and entered into his palace. There he prepared a banquet at which he entertained his friends in honour of his victory over the great bull. After the banquet the guests reclined upon their couches and slept. During Ea-bani's sleep he saw a vision, and when he awoke in the morning he drew nigh to Gilgamesh and began to tell him of the things which he had seen.

The Seventh Tablet begins with Ea-bani's account of his dream, but so few fragments of the text of this and the following tablet have been preserved that it is not possible to follow the course of the narrative at this point. All we know for certain is that Ea-bani's death occurs at the end of the Eighth Tablet. He seems to have received a wound in battle, but in what manner and at the hands of what foe, we cannot say. All that we can gather from the mutilated text is that he was laid low upon his bed with the sickness which resulted from his wound. For twelve days he lay sick, and having summoned Gilgamesh to his bedside, and having told him the manner in which he had received his wound, he died. We may reasonably conjecture that his death was brought about by Ishtar, whose anger he had aroused. Gilgamesh himself escaped from death, but we find he had been smitten with a sore sickness, which no doubt was also due to the anger of the great goddess whose love he had scorned.

The Ninth Tablet opens with the lament of Gilgamesh for the death of his friend, and with his resolve to seek out his ancestor, Tsît-napishtim, who might perhaps help him to escape a similar fate. The tablet begins as follows :—

"For his friend Ea-bani
"Gilgamesh wept bitterly and he lay stretched out upon the ground.
"(He cried): 'Let me not die like Ea-bani!
"Grief hath entered into my body, and
"I fear death, and I lie stretched out upon the ground.
"To (test) the power of Tsît-napishtim, son of Ubara-Tutu,
"I will set out, and I will not tarry by the way.'"

Gilgamesh describes his journey thus :—

"To a mountain gorge I came by night,
"Lions I beheld, and I was terrified.
"I raised my head and I prayed to the Moon-god,
"And to the [chief] of the gods came my cry,
"[And he hearkened and] showed favour unto me."

From what remains of the text it appears that Gilgamesh had a dream in which the Moon-god shewed him the way by which he might safely pass over the mountains. Gilgamesh succeeded in crossing the first mountain range which barred his path, and he next came to a still greater mountain named Māshu, that is to say, the Mountain of the Sunset. The poem continues as follows:—

"Then he came to the Mountain of Māshu,
"The portals of which are guarded daily [by monsters];
"Their backs mount up to the rampart of heaven,
"And their fore parts reach down beneath Arallū.
"Scorpion-men guard the gate (of Māshu);
"They strike terror [into men], and it is death to behold them.
"Their splendour is great, for it overwhelms the mountains;
"From sunrise to sunset they guard the Sun.
"Gilgamesh beheld them,
"And his face grew dark with fear and terror,
"And the wildness of their aspect robbed him of his senses."

One of the Scorpion-men then caught sight of Gilgamesh, and, turning to his wife, told her that the body of the man they saw approaching resembled that of a god. His wife replied that Gilgamesh was partly divine and partly human. The Scorpion-man then told her how Gilgamesh had set out on his long journey in accordance with the will of the gods, and he described the steep mountains which he had already crossed. Gilgamesh, seeing that the monster regarded him with friendly eyes, recovered from his fright, and told him of the purpose of his journey, namely, to go to Tsīt-napishtim, his ancestor, who stood in the assembly of the gods, and had the power over life and death. The Scorpion-man replied by describing the difficulties and dangers which he would encounter if he persisted in his purpose of traversing the Mountain of Māshu, adding that for twelve *kasbu*, that is, for a space of twenty-four hours, he would have to pass through thick darkness. But Gilgamesh was not discouraged. The Scorpion-man, therefore, yielded to his request, and opened the gate of the mountain and let him through.

For twenty-four hours Gilgamesh marched onwards, "and the darkness was thick and there was no light." But at the end of this long and dreadful journey he came out once more into the light of the sun, and the first thing he beheld was a beautiful and wonderful tree. The poem describes the tree in the following words :—

"Precious stones it bore as fruit,
"Branches hung from it which were beautiful to behold.
"The top of the tree was *lapis lazuli*,
"And it was laden with fruit which dazzled the eye of him that beheld."

This tree grew in a great park or orchard beside

other trees which were also laden with precious stones; but Gilgamesh did not tarry among the trees nor stop to gather their fruit. The shore of the sea was not far off and he wished to lose no time in reaching it, for he knew that he must cross the sea to reach Tsīt-napishtim his ancestor.

The text of the Tenth Tablet reveals to us Gilgamesh involved in further troubles. The sea-coast, to which he had now come, was ruled over by a princess named Sabitu, who dwelt in a palace by the shore. She beheld Gilgamesh from afar, and, as he drew near, she went into her palace and shut the door. Without her assistance, however, Gilgamesh could not cross the sea, so he went up to her door and demanded why she had shut it, and threatened that if she did not open it he would break it down. A gap in the text prevents us from knowing Sabitu's answer to this threat. When the text is again continuous we find Gilgamesh telling Sabitu the reason of his journey, namely, that he may learn how to escape the fate of his friend Ea-bani; he ended by asking her the way to the abode of Tsīt-napishtim, saying—

"[Tell me] O Sabitu, which is the way to Tsīt-napishtim?
"If it is possible, I will cross the sea.
"But if it is not possible, I will lie me down upon the ground in despair."

Sabitu replied, saying—

ARAD-EA, THE SAILOR.

"O Gilgamesh, there hath never been a ferry (here),
"Neither hath any one ever crossed the sea.
"The hero Shamash hath crossed the sea, but, besides Shamash, who can cross it?
"The crossing is difficult, the way is very hard,
"The Waters of Death are shut in (?), they are closed up as with a bolt.
"O Gilgamesh, how canst thou cross the sea?
"And if thou shouldst come to the Waters of Death, what wouldst thou do?"

Sabitu, however, told Gilgamesh that there was one who might perhaps help him, namely, Arad-Ea, the sailor who served Tsīt-napishtim. To him she sent him and told him to ask Arad-Ea to take him across. If he refused, Gilgamesh would have to turn back.

Gilgamesh sought out Arad-Ea and told him of his grief, and of the reason of his journey; he then made the request that he would show him the way to Tsīt-napishtim, and ended his demand with the words he had already used to Sabitu, saying—

"If it is possible, I will cross the sea,
"But if it is not possible, I will lie me down upon the ground in despair."

Arad-Ea consented to make the journey, and told Gilgamesh to go into the wood and cut down a tree out of which he might make a large rudder for the ship, since they would need special tackle for the voyage. The poem then describes how they made their preparations and set out on their journey, as follows—

"Gilgamesh on hearing this (*i.e.*, Arad-Ea's instructions)

"Took his axe in his hand . . . .

"And he went into the wood and [cut] a rudder, five measures in length,

"And he smeared it all over with pitch.

"Gilgamesh and Arad-Ea then went up into [the ship].

"The ship was thrust out into the waves, and they began their voyage.

Gilgamesh and Arad-Ea crossing the ocean and the "Waters of Death." On the left of the picture is a representation of Gilgamesh and Ea-bani in conflict with a lion. (From a cylinder-seal in the British Museum, No. 89,588.)

"A course of one month and five days within three days [did they accomplish],

"And thus Arad-Ea arrived at the Waters of Death."

To pass over the Waters of Death was a task attended with difficulty and danger, and Arad-Ea needed all the help that Gilgamesh could give him to steer the ship in safety. After they had made the passage, Gilgamesh loosened his girdle and rested from his exertions. Then they drew nigh the shore of the land where

Tsīt-napishtim and his wife dwelt apart from mankind. Tsīt-napishtim beheld Gilgamesh afar off and marvelled to see a living man cross the Waters of Death. Gilgamesh then approached the shore and, while still sitting in the ship, he explained to Tsīt-napishtim the reason he had sought him out. He told him of his adventures with Ea-bani, and he described the sad death of his friend and his own grief at his loss. He recounted how he had set out to seek help from Tsīt-napishtim, and how on his journey he had passed over steep mountains and crossed dangerous seas. He ended his long recital by asking his ancestor how he might escape the sad fate of death that had overtaken Ea-bani his friend.

Tsīt-napishtim was grieved at the words of Gilgamesh, but told him he could do nothing to help him to escape from death. He told him that death comes to all, and that no man could escape from it,

" As long as houses are built, . . .
" And as long as brethren quarrel,
" And as long as there is hatred in the land,
" And as long as the river beareth its waters [to the sea]."

He added that the gods whose lot it is to decree death pass sentence when they will, and that no man could tell when his own time might come. And he said—

" The Anunnaki, the great gods, decree fate,
" And with them Mammetum, the maker of destiny,

"And they determine death and life,
"But the days of death are not known."

With these words the Tenth Tablet of the poem ends.

On the Eleventh Tablet Gilgamesh asked Tsĭt-napishtim the reason of his own escape from death. He gazed upon him, and, seeing that his appearance was like that of a living man, said—

"I behold thee, O Tsĭt-napishtim,
"But thy appearance is not changed. As I am, so art thou also.
"Yea, thou art not changed. As I am, so art thou also."

He then asked him the reason, saying,

"[Tell me], How didst thou obtain the life which thou dost enjoy in the assembly of the gods?"

In reply to this question, Tsĭt-napishtim told Gilgamesh the story of the deluge, which has been already described in Chapter IV.

During the telling of the story, Gilgamesh sat listening at a little distance from the shore in the ship, for, sore-smitten as he was with sickness, he was not able to go up from the ship. When Tsĭt-napishtim had finished the tale of his own adventures he turned to the hero and promised to restore him to health, for that at least he could do, though he could not show him a way to escape from death when his time should come. As a first step towards the recovery Tsĭt-napishtim bade him sleep. For six days and six nights Gilgamesh continued to sit in the ship, and at the end of that time sleep came upon him suddenly "like a storm." While Gilgamesh slept, Tsīt-napishtim told his wife to prepare some magic food, which she administered unto him while he slept. On awaking from his sleep Gilgamesh felt that he was enchanted, and asked what had been done to him, and they told him of the magical food which had been prepared and which he had eaten. To complete his cure Tsīt-napishtim caused Arad-Ea to carry Gilgamesh to a certain fountain where he washed his sores in the healing waters, and he was cleansed from his terrible disease. When he was about to depart on his homeward journey, the wife of Tsīt-napishtim asked her husband what they could give him to ensure his safe return to his own land. Although Tsīt-napishtim had already told Gilgamesh that no man could escape from death, yet now, as the latter was preparing to take his leave, he disclosed to him the existence of a magic plant which had the power of prolonging life. Gilgamesh then set sail in company with Arad-Ea to go and search for the plant. They succeeded in finding it, and Gilgamesh joyfully cried that he would carry it to Erech with him, and that by eating it he would regain his youth. Gilgamesh and Arad-Ea then turned back carrying the plant with them. And when they had journeyed thirty *kasbu*, they came to a brook wherein flowed cool and refreshing water. And when

Gilgamesh went down to the brook to drink, a demon in the form of a serpent darted out and carried away the plant. Gilgamesh bitterly lamented the loss of the plant, but could do nothing to recover it. He therefore continued his journey and in due time returned to Erech. With this incident the Eleventh Tablet closes.

The Twelfth Tablet of the poem relates how Gilgamesh, after his return from his long journey, continued to lament for Ea-bani. He called to mind the common acts of daily life, which his friend could no longer perform, now that he was imprisoned in the underworld, and addressing Ea-bani he said—

"Thou canst no longer stretch thy bow upon the earth;

"And those who were slain with the bow are round about thee.

"Thou canst no longer bear a sceptre in thy hand;

"And the spirits of the dead have taken thee captive.

"Thou canst no longer wear shoes upon thy feet;

"Thou canst no longer raise thy war-cry on the earth.

"No more dost thou kiss thy wife whom thou didst love;

"No more dost thou smite thy wife whom thou didst hate.

"No more dost thou kiss thy daughter whom thou didst love;

"No more dost thou smite thy daughter whom thou didst hate.

"The sorrow of the Underworld hath taken hold upon thee."

Gilgamesh then appealed to the gods to help him in his sorrow and to enable him to again behold his friend. With this object he went alone into the temple of the god Bēl, and, addressing him as his "father," told him of his trouble; but Bēl could not help him. He next told his sorrow to Sin, the Moon-god, but he too could do nothing for him; and Ea, to whom he next appealed, could do naught to help him. Last of all he besought Nergal, the god of the dead, to use his power and to restore Ea-bani to him. On hearing the prayer of Gilgamesh, Nergal granted his request. He opened the ground, and "caused the spirit of Ea-bani to come "forth from the earth like a wind."

Gilgamesh thereupon asked Ea-bani to describe to him the underworld, crying, "Tell me, my friend, tell "me; tell me the appearance of the land which thou "hast seen." But Ea-bani replied, "I cannot tell thee, "my friend, I cannot tell thee." This refusal to speak of the abode of the dead was not due to any command laid upon Ea-bani not to reveal such matters to the living, but was prompted by his grief at the dreariness of the region from which he had just been released. After bidding Gilgamesh sit down and weep, he proceeded to describe the underworld as an abode of misery, where was the worm which devoured, and where all was cloaked in dust. The text is here imperfect, but the closing lines of the tablet which contain the end of Ea-bani's description of the condition of the dead are preserved. In this passage Ea-bani contrasts the lot of the warrior, who has received due burial, with that of the man whose corpse is left uncared for on the field, in the following words :—

"On a couch he lieth
  "And drinketh pure water,
"The man who was slain in battle—thou and I have
    oft seen such an one.
"His father and his mother [support] his head,
  "And his wife [kneeleth] at his side.
"But the man whose corpse is cast upon the field—
  "Thou and I have oft seen such an one—
"His spirit resteth not in the earth.
"The man whose spirit has none to care for it—
  "Thou and I have oft seen such an one—
"The dregs of the vessel, the leavings of the feast,
  "And that which is cast out upon the street, are
    his food."

With these words the poem comes to an end.

We have followed the exploits of the hero Gilgamesh as they are told on the tablets from Ashur-bāni-pal's library, and from their varied nature it is clear that they have been drawn from many different sources. What historical foundation may underlie the tales told

COMPOSITION OF THE POEM.

of this early king of Erech we cannot say, but it is legitimate to suppose that some early ruler did perform acts of valour in the past, and that his name has formed a centre around which stories and legends gathered in the course of centuries. To separate the different narratives which have been combined to form the poem as we know it would scarcely repay the trouble of analysis, but a bare enumeration of the principal sections of the story will suffice to show its composite nature. The rule of Gilgamesh in Erech, the story of Ukhat and Ea-bani, the expedition against Khumbaba, the love of the goddess Ishtar for Gilgamesh, the slaying of the monstrous bull, the journey of Gilgamesh to the Mountain of the Sunset, the passage of the Waters of Death, Tsīt-napishtim's story of the Deluge, the search for the Plant of Life, and the recall of Ea-bani's spirit from the underworld—such are the chief sections into which the poem falls. Of these the account of the deluge is the section most loosely connected with the story of Gilgamesh, but other sections of the poem, which have been more skilfully interwoven, were doubtless at one time entirely independent of the narrative.

We may assume that many of these tales go back to hoary antiquity, and that in the course of time they became associated with the name of Gilgamesh, having previously been associated with the names of other heroes. It is interesting to note that as Gilgamesh was thus credited with adventures that were not his by right, so at a later time some of his exploits were borrowed to add lustre to the fame of another popular hero, Alexander the Great. As Gilgamesh set out to learn the secret of immortality, and in the course of his journey came to the Mountain of Māshu, and passed through a region of thick darkness, and crossed the Waters of Death, so Alexander is said to have journeyed in search of the Waters of Life, and to have come to a mountain called Mūsās or Māsīs, and to have passed through the land of darkness, and to have crossed the fœtid sea.[1] This journey of Gilgamesh, moreover, in consequence of its being ascribed to Alexander in the text of Pseudo-Callisthenes, has found an echo in the Koran.[2]

Of the various sections of the great Babylonian poem describing the deeds of Gilgamesh the most interesting portions are perhaps those towards the end in which Ea-bani talks with Gilgamesh after the release of the former from the underworld; for from these passages we gain some information with regard to the conceptions formed by the Babylonians of a future life. Another of the principal legends of the Babylonians recounts how the goddess Ishtar once left the earth and descended into the underworld, and the poem in

---

[1] See Budge, *The History of Alexander the Great*, pp. 148, 171 ff., and *The Life and Exploits of Alexander the Great*, Vol. I., pp. xl. f. Meissner, *Alexander und Gilgamos*, pp. 4 ff.

[2] Sûra, xviii.

which this legend has been preserved enables us to augment the fragments of Ea-bani's description of the dead that have come down to us.[1] The poem describing the descent of the goddess begins as follows:—

"To the land whence none return, the place of darkness,
"Ishtar the daughter of Sin inclined her ear.[2]
"The daughter of Sin inclined her ear
"To the house of darkness, the seat of the god Irkalla,
"To the house from which none who enter come forth again,
"To the road whose course returns not,
"To the house wherein he who enters is excluded from the light,
"To the place where dust is their bread, and mud their food.
"They behold not the light, they dwell in darkness,
"And are clothed like birds in a garment of feathers;
"And over door and bolt the dust is scattered.
"When Ishtar drew near the gate of the land whence none return,
"She spake to the porter at the gate:
"'Ho! Porter! Open thy gate!
"Open thy gate that I may enter in.

---

[1] Cf. Jeremias, *Die babylonisch-assyrischen Vorstellungen vom Leben nach dem Tode*, pp. 10 ff.
[2] *I.e.*, turned her attention.

"If thou openest not thy gate, so that I may not enter,
"I will smite the door, I will shatter the bolt,
"I will smite the threshold and tear down the doors,
"I will raise up the dead, that they may devour the living,
"And the dead shall outnumber those that live.'
"The porter opened his mouth,
"And addressed the mighty Ishtar:
"'Stay, O Lady, do not throw it down.
"Let me go and declare thy name to the queen Allatu.'"

The porter then went to Allatu, the queen of the underworld, and told her of Ishtar's coming; but Allatu was angered at the news and wept for Ishtar's victims, and she bade the porter admit her, saying—

"Go, porter, open thy gate for her,
"And take possession of her according to the ancient laws."

The poem then describes how Ishtar was admitted, and how she was gradually stripped of her clothing, in the following words:—

"The porter went and opened his gate for her, (saying),
"'Enter, O Lady, let Cuthah [1] be glad at [thee].

---

[1] In Cuthah was E-shidlam, the great temple of Nergal the god of the dead; the name of the city is here used as a synonym for the underworld.

"Let the palace of the land whence none return rejoice before thee.'

"The First Gate he made her enter, . . . and he took the great crown from off her head.

"'Why, O porter, didst thou take the great crown from off my head?'

"'Enter, O Lady, for thus are the laws of Allatu.'"

In this manner was Ishtar made to pass through each of the seven gates of the underworld. At every gate an article of her apparel was removed, and to her remonstrances the porter always made the same reply, bidding her pass through the gate, for such were the laws of Allatu. Thus, naked and powerless, she was brought into Allatu's presence. The queen of the underworld did not receive her with favour, and commanded Namtar, the demon of the plague, to strike her with disease in all the members of her body.

But Ishtar was not left for ever in the clutches of Allatu. The absence of the goddess of love from the earth soon brought disaster upon men and beasts, for they no longer felt the desires of the body, and all creatures ceased to perform their natural functions. News of this calamity was carried to Shamash the Sun-god by Pap-sukal, the minister of the gods, and Shamash hastened to Sin and to Ea to consult with them as to what measures should be taken to remedy this state of things. Ea thereupon created a being named Uddushu-nāmir, whom he sent down to the underworld to procure the release of Ishtar. Following Ea's instructions Uddushu-namir obtained admittance to the underworld and appeared before Allatu. He conjured her by the power of the great gods to grant him the Waters of Life, by means of which he intended to restore Ishtar to life. Allatu was enraged at the request, and, although she could not resist the power he had invoked on behalf of Ishtar, she wreaked her

Representation upon a Babylonian cylinder-seal of the goddess Ishtar and other deities. In the centre is Shamash, the sun-god, rising on the horizon. On his right, by the side of a sacred tree, stands the goddess Ishtar, with outstretched wings. On her right is a god holding a bow and a lion, and on her left are a river-god and another deity. The name of the owner of the seal, written to the left of the picture, is "Adda, the scribe." (British Museum, No. 89,115.)

vengeance upon him and cursed him with a terrible curse. She then turned to Namtar and told him to bring Ishtar forth and sprinkle over her the Waters of Life. When this had been done Ishtar was led out through the seven gates of the underworld, and at each of the gates the article of her apparel that had previously been taken from her was restored. Thus was she brought back again to earth.

In the actual text of the legend we are not told Ishtar's motive in descending into the underworld, but we may perhaps see a reference to it in the last few lines of the poem. Considerable doubt exists with regard to the interpretation of these lines, but it seems clear that they are not a continuation of the narrative and that they were intended to be addressed to the persons who may be supposed to have heard the poem recited—perhaps to certain mourners for the dead. In this exhortation the reciter refers to Tammuz, the spouse of Ishtar's youth, and he bids his hearers pour out pure water in his honour and offer him goodly oil. A little further on a reference is made to "the day of "Tammuz" as a time when male and female mourners made lamentation and when incense was burnt. It may be conjectured therefore that the motive of the goddess in descending to the underworld was to bring back her youthful husband from the dead, and the poem in the form in which we have it would in that case contain only a part of the original legend. This story of the goddess Ishtar was possibly recited at the annual festival held in commemoration of the death of Tammuz, when women mourned for the dead god in Babylonia, as they mourned for him at Jerusalem in the time of the prophet Ezekiel.[1]

We have seen that a portion of the poem of Gilgamesh, and the legend of the goddess Ishtar, contained

[1] Ezek. viii. 14.

descriptions and stories of the underworld; for the underworld was a mysterious abode about which legends would naturally gather. Heaven was also a place of mystery, and it is not surprising that stories of heroes who had journeyed thither should also find a place in Babylonian mythology. One such story is told of an old Babylonian hero named Etana, who, with the help of his friend the Eagle, succeeded in penetrating into heaven. A series of tablets existed in Ashur-bāni-pal's library, which recounted the deeds of Etana,[1] and on most of the fragments that remain the Eagle appears as Etana's friend and comrade. On one occasion, when the wife of Etana was about to bear him a son, but could not bring the child to the birth, the Eagle helped Etana to procure the "Plant of Birth" which would ensure a safe delivery. On another occasion the Eagle carried Etana up to heaven. The hero clung to the Eagle's wings, and they mounted together till they could see the gates of heaven. As they drew near to the Gate of Anu, Bēl, and Ea and to the Gate of Sin, Shamash, Rammān, and Ishtar, they beheld a throne of great splendour, and Etana was afraid and cast himself down at the foot of the throne. But the Eagle encouraged Etana to mount with him still higher and they again set out. After every two

---

[1] The legends of Etana have been edited by E. T. Harper, *Beiträge zur Assyriologie*, Bd. II., pp. 391 ff., and Morris Jastrow, *op. cit.*, Bd. III., pp. 363 ff.

hours of his flight, the Eagle pointed to the earth below them, which grew smaller and smaller as they ascended, and at length they reached the Gate of Anu, Bēl, and Ea. After resting for a while the Eagle proposed to Etana that he should carry him up still higher to the dwelling of the goddess Ishtar. Again they set out, but when they had flown for six hours Etana cried to the Eagle to stop. What misfortune then overtook the pair we do not know, for the text of the legend is broken; what still remains, however, recounts that they fell headlong through the air and were dashed upon the ground.[1]

[1] Another portion of the story of Etana refers to the subsequent fate of the Eagle; and it may here be described as it illustrates a class of Babylonian myths in which beasts and birds are represented as talking like men, and appealing to the gods for help and advice. The story tells how the Eagle incurred the hatred of the Serpent, and how the latter, with the help of the Sun-god, took his revenge. The story begins with the following lines:—
"His heart prompted the Eagle . . . ,
"He considered, and his heart [prompted him . . .]
"To eat the young of his companion . . .
"The Eagle opened his mouth and spake unto his young, saying,
"'The young of the Serpent will I eat . . .
"I will ascend and [mount up] into heaven;
"I will swoop down upon the top of a tree and I will eat (the Serpent's) brood.'
"One of the young birds who was endowed with much wisdom, addressed the Eagle, his father:
"'Do not eat, O my father, (for) the net of Shamash is laid.
"The snare and the ban of Shamash will fall upon thee and will catch thee.
"Whoso transgresseth the law of Shamash, will Shamash terribly [requite].'
"But he did not hearken to them, and gave no heed to the word of his young one.

From the portion of the legend quoted in the note we learn the Eagle's fate, but we are not told what became of his friend, the hero Etana. Etana must

"He swooped down and ate the young of the Serpent."

The Serpent then repaired to Shamash the Sun god, who as judge of heaven and earth could not allow such a wrong to go unpunished, and he told him his story and appealed to him for justice. He described how his nest was set in a tree and how the Eagle espied it, and devoured his young, saying:—

"He swooped down and ate [my young ones]!
"[Behold], O Shamash, the evil he hath done me.
"Help, O Shamash! Thy net is like unto the broad earth;
"Thy snare is like unto the distant heaven!
"Who hath ever escaped from thy net?
"Even Zū, the worker of evil, who raised the head of evil, [did not escape]!"

The story of Zū which is here referred to by the Serpent has been partly recovered from other tablets from Ashur-bāni-pal's library, and is described later on in this chapter. We there read of Zū's treachery, and how he stole the Tablets of Destiny from Anu, and how he escaped with them to his mountain home. From the Serpent's reference to his fate we gather that the Sun-god succeeded in catching and punishing him. In the story of the Serpent and the Eagle, Shamash does not himself punish the Eagle, but explains to the Serpent a device by which he may obtain vengeance. The narrative continues:—

["When he had listened to] the prayer of the Serpent,
"Shamash opened his mouth and to [the Serpent spake]:
"'Take the road and go [into the mountain],
"And hide thyself in a wild [ox that is dead].
"Open its bowels, [tear open its belly],
"And take up thy dwelling [in its belly].
"[All] the birds of heaven [shall swoop down],
"And . . . .
"The Eagle [shall come] with them,
"And not knowing [thy plot (?)],
"He will seek a piece of the flesh, moving swiftly,
"And making for the hidden parts.
"When he hath entered into the midst, do thou seize him by his wing,

have incurred the anger of the gods by attempting to mount to their abode, and it is possible that he was dashed to pieces when he fell with the Eagle to the ground from the height of heaven.

" Tear off his wings, his pinions, and his claws,
" Pull him in pieces and cast him into a pit, . . .
" That he may die a death from hunger and thirst.'
" At the word of Shamash, the hero, the Serpent departed and went into the mountain.
" And the Serpent came upon a wild ox,
" And he opened its bowels, he tore open its belly,
" And he took up his dwelling in its belly.
" All the birds of heaven swooped down and ate of the flesh.
" But the Eagle (at first) suspected his evil purpose,
" And with the flock of birds did not eat of the flesh.
" Then the Eagle opened his mouth and spake unto his young:
" 'Come ! let us swoop down, and let us also eat of the flesh of this wild ox !'
" One of the young birds, who was endowed with much wisdom,
" To turn aside [his] father . . . spake :
[" ' O my Father], the Serpent lurks in [the flesh of] this wild ox !'

. . . .

" But he did not hearken to them, and gave no heed to the word of his young one.
" He swooped down and stood upon the wild ox.
" The Eagle . . . examined the flesh, he looked about carefully before and behind him.
" He again examined the flesh, he looked about carefully before and behind him.
" Then, moving swiftly, he made for the hidden parts.
" When he had entered into the midst, the serpent seized him by his wing."

So far everything had fallen out as the Sun-god had foretold. The Eagle, now that he sees he is in his enemy's power, begs for mercy, and tries to bribe the Serpent. But the latter reminds him that an appeal to Shamash is irrevocable, and that if he did not carry out the Sun-god's bidding, he would himself share in the punishment which he now inflicts.

" The Eagle opened [his mouth] and spake to the Serpent :

ADAPA AND THE SOUTH WIND.

A legend is told of another ancient hero, named Adapa, who also journeyed to heaven, but in this case the hero did not seek to get there by his own devices, but was summoned thither by Anu, the god of heaven. The legend is preserved on one of the tablets that was found at Tell el-Amarna,[1] and, in the form in which we have it, dates from the first half of the fifteenth century before Christ.

The story narrates that Adapa, the son of Ea, was one day out on the sea in a boat, engaged in catching fish for his father's house. Suddenly Shûtu, the South wind, blew and upset his boat and threw him into the water. Adapa was furious at this outrage, so he caught the South wind by her wings and broke them. In this passage the South wind is pictured as a winged female monster, and it is possible that in other respects also she was thought to resemble a bird. We have no representation of her, but it may be inferred that she was a creature of unprepossessing appearance, for the South wind was dreaded by the Babylonians

---

"'Have mercy upon me, and I will present thee with a gift according to thy pleasure.'
"The Serpent opened his mouth and spake to the Eagle:
"'If I release thee, Shamash will . . . against us,
"And thy punishment will be transferred to me,
"Which now, as a punishment, I execute on thee.'
"So he tore off his wings, his pinions, and his talons,
"He pulled him in pieces and cast him into a pit, . . .
"And he died a death from hunger and thirst."

[1] See above, p. 118 f.; cf. Harper, *Beiträge zur Assyriologie*, Bd. II., pp. 418 ff.

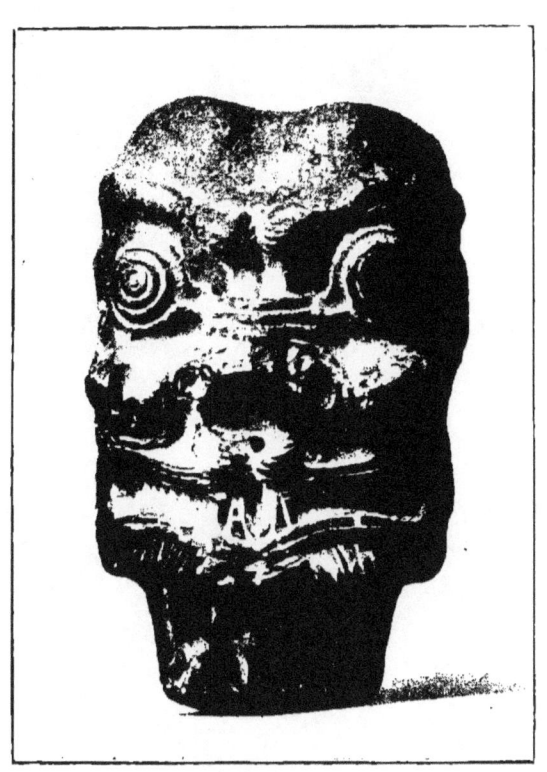

Head of the demon of the South-west wind. (British Museum, No. 22,459.)

inasmuch as it caused destructive floods in the low-lying regions of the Euphrates valley. The accompanying illustration of a kindred spirit, the demon of the South-west wind, is taken from a marble head in the British Museum, and it well represents the hideous conception formed by the Babylonians of the monster who caused destructive storms and tempests.

When Adapa had broken Shūtu's wings, the South wind was no longer able to blow over the earth. After seven days had passed, Anu, the god of heaven, asked his minister Ilabrat why the South wind had ceased to blow, and he told him that Adapa had broken her wings. Anu thereupon summoned Adapa to heaven to answer the charge. Before he set out Adapa received instructions from his father Ea, who told him how, by putting on garments of mourning, he would propitiate Tammuz and Gishzida, the two gods who stood at the gate of heaven, and who, if approached with due deference, would secure for him a favourable reception before Anu. Ea also warned him that after he entered Anu's presence they would offer him "Meat of Death" and "Water of Death"; neither of these was he to touch. They would then bring him a garment and oil, and these he need not avoid; the garment he might put on and with the oil he might anoint himself.

On arriving at the gate of heaven Adapa duly secured the favour of Tammuz and Gishzida and was led into Anu's presence. Anu asked him why he had broken the wings of the South wind, and Adapa related how the South wind had upset his boat while he was fishing on the sea. Tammuz and Gishzida then interposed on Adapa's behalf, and at their words Anu's anger against Adapa was turned away. Then Anu, having pardoned Adapa for his offence, decided that, as he had seen the interior of heaven, he must be added to the company of the gods. He therefore commanded that they should bring Adapa "Meat of "Life" that he might eat. But Adapa would not eat the "Meat of Life"; neither would he drink the "Water of Life" which was next placed before him. But when they brought him a garment he put it on, and when they offered him oil he anointed himself therewith. And Anu, when he saw that Adapa had not partaken of the "Meat of Life" and the "Water "of Life," asked him, saying, "Come, Adapa, why "dost thou neither eat nor drink? For now thou "canst not live." And Adapa answered that he had refused to eat and drink, because Ea his lord had so commanded him. The reason which prompted Ea to lay these injunctions upon his son seems to have been that he feared the gods would seek to slay Adapa. Anu, on the other hand, decided to make Adapa immortal, and did not offer him deadly food as Ea had predicted. Thus Adapa, through his father's suspicions, missed the privilege of enjoying immortality.

In the legends of Etana and Adapa we have stories of mortals who by presumptuous acts brought themselves into conflict with the gods. Among the gods themselves, however, ambition was not absent, and in the legend of Zū we read how one of the lesser deities aimed at obtaining the control of the whole company of the gods.[1] It will be remembered that Marduk was identified in course of time with the older god Bēl, or Enlil,[2] and in the great legend of the creation we are told that he captured the Tablets of Destiny from Kingu, the captain of the host of Tiāmat. In the following legend we read how at a later time Zū stole them from Bēl and carried them off to his mountain. The legend runs as follows:—

"His eyes beheld the symbols of Bēl's dominion,
"The crown of his sovereignty, and the robe of his godhead.
"Zū gazed at his divine Tablets of Destiny,
"And he gazed at the father of the gods, the god of Duranki,
"And a longing for Bēl's dominion was held fast in his heart.
"'I will take the Tablets of the gods,
"And I will direct the oracles of all the gods.
"I will establish my throne and dispense my commands.
"I will rule all the Spirits of Heaven.'

[1] See Harper, *op. cit.*, pp. 408 ff.   [2] See above, pp. 18 ff.

"And his heart meditated battle
"At the entrance of the hall, where he beheld as he waited the dawn of the day.
"Now when Bēl was pouring out the clear water,
"And his diadem was taken off and lay upon the throne,
"(Zū) seized the Tablets of Destiny,
"He took Bēl's dominion, the power of giving commands.
"Then Zū fled away and hid himself in his mountain."

The gods were dismayed at the theft, and Bēl strode through the hall in rage. Then Anu, the god of heaven, addressed the gods, his sons, and called for a champion, who should recover the Tablets. Thereupon the gods called upon Rammān to be their champion, and Anu promised him honour and power should he succeed. But Rammān refused the offer, as did also two other deities when asked. Who eventually conquered Zū and recovered the Tablets is not quite certain, for the end of the legend is missing. From a passage in the legend of Etana, however, it may be conjectured that the Sun-god undertook the task, and vanquished Zū by catching him in his net.

Such are the principal legends and stories, as far as we know them, that were told in Babylonia concerning the gods and the heroes of olden time. That they were not idle tales, but had a religious significance for the people among whom we find them, is what might be inferred from a comparison of them with the mythologies of other nations. We have, moreover, evidence to this effect in some of the poems that have been already described. In the poem which recounts the descent of Ishtar into the underworld, we saw reason to believe that it was recited in connection with the yearly festival held in commemoration of the death of Tammuz. The introduction to the long poem which records the history of Gilgamesh stated that a knowledge of the hero's achievements would bring prosperity to the man who made himself acquainted with them, and it is probable that this statement was not regarded as a mere conventional preface, but was implicitly believed. It is true that in the legend we are not told that Gilgamesh was raised to the company of the gods, but he was undoubtedly regarded as a god in popular belief. There is a prayer in the British Museum [1] in which a sick man beseeches Gilgamesh to cure him of his sickness, and he addresses him as the "perfect king, the judge of "the Anunnaki, the great arbiter among men who "orders the four quarters of heaven, the governor "of the world, and the lord of the regions of the "earth"; the sick man also exclaims, "Thou art a "judge, and like unto a god thou givest decisions." It is clear therefore that to Gilgamesh was ascribed

[1] Sm. 1371 + Sm. 1877.

no small authority and power. The estimation in which both he and the hero Etana were held is also attested by the fact that the determinative for "god" is always placed before their names.

A further piece of evidence that these mythological compositions were put to very practical uses is afforded by certain tablets which have been found inscribed with legends concerning the chief Plague-god of the Babylonians,[1] describing the destruction which he and his attendant deity Ishum spread upon the earth. Both gods are therein pictured as warriors who held bloody sway in the cities of Babylonia, and undertook military expeditions into distant lands. These legends are inscribed on several tablets, and the last one of the series recounts how the anger of the Plague-god was at length appeased, and ends with a speech of the Plague-god, in which he promises protection and prosperity to all those who make known his wondrous deeds. He continues, " Should I be angry, and should "the seven-fold god cause destruction; the dagger of "pestilence shall not approach the house wherein this "tablet is set, and it shall remain unharmed." This last section of the poem, including the passage just quoted, has been found on two interesting tablets in the British Museum.[2] At the top of each tablet is a small projection in which a hole has been bored, and

---

[1] The name of this god is generally read as Dibbarra, though Ura and Girra are also possible readings.
[2] See *Zeitschrift für Assyriologie*, Bd. xi. pp. 50 ff.

through it was passed a cord by which it might be suspended. There is no doubt that these tablets were hung up in the entrance of a house, and that they served as amulets for keeping off the plague. Thus there are many indications that the myths and legends of the gods played an important part in the practical religion and worship of the Babylonians.

To decide in what manner these various legends of the gods arose, and to trace the changes which they underwent in the long course of Babylonian history, would result in an interesting, but certainly a very speculative, enquiry. Conjecture, based mainly on the internal evidence furnished by the myths themselves in the forms in which they have come down to us, naturally cannot lead to very definite results; but one broad conclusion may be drawn from a study of the tablets with at least some probability of its being correct. It can hardly be disputed that changes in the aspect of nature suggested many of the legends about the gods. Perhaps the clearest instance of this explanation of natural processes by legend is presented in the legends of the Plague-god; the campaigns he undertook, and the bloody battles he waged, were doubtless suggested by the ravages of disease which were regarded as his handiwork. The descent of Ishtar into the underworld and the languishing of all nature in consequence, which was followed by her restoration to earth and the renewal of the powers of men and beasts, was clearly intended to explain the decay of nature in the autumn, and the quickening of the earth in the spring. Zū's treacherous usurpation of Bēl's sovereignty may perhaps be based on the sudden overwhelming of the sun by storm and clouds.

There is another element in many of these legends which must not be lost sight of, and that is the substratum of historical fact which underlies the story, and was the nucleus around which it gathered. Echoes from the history of the remote past may perhaps be traced in such episodes as the expedition of Gilgamesh and Ea-bani against Khumbaba king of Elam, as well as in some of the conflicts described in the Plague-god legends. The growth of legends around the figures of prominent heroes is common in every race that has a history, and this was particularly the case in Babylonia. A number of legends, for instance, have come down to us concerning certain ancient Babylonian kings, of whose historical existence we have abundant proof from other sources. Sargon I. was an actual king, who ruled in the city of Agade about B.C. 3800, and many of whose inscriptions have recently been found at Nippur. Yet we possess a legend concerning this monarch, in which he tells how his mother set him floating on the Euphrates in a basket made of rushes, how Akki the gardener rescued him and brought him up as his own son, and how while he was still a gardener the goddess Ishtar loved him and eventually set him over the kingdom which he ruled. The text of the legend of Sargon was a long one, but little more than this story of his youth has been preserved. It will at least suffice to show how myth and legend gathered around the figures of famous kings and heroes of old time. The legend of Sargon is not a solitary example of this process. The so-called "Cuthæan "legend of Creation" describes a legend of an early king of Cuthah,[1] and fragments of similar myths have been found in Ashur-bāni-pal's library which recount the legendary deeds of Narām-Sin, the son of Sargon, who lived about B.C. 3750, and of Dungi, king of Ur, about B.C. 2500, and of Khammurabi, king of Babylon, about B.C. 2200, and of Nebuchadnezzar I., king of Babylon about B.C. 1120. The tablets which contain these legends are very fragmentary, but they illustrate the process by which historical personages in course of time became demi-gods and legendary heroes.

[1] See above, pp. 92 ff.

CHAPTER VI.

THE DUTY OF MAN TO HIS GOD AND TO HIS NEIGHBOUR.

In the three preceding chapters the principal legends and myths that have been found in Babylonian literature have been described, and the extracts which have been quoted from them will have enabled the reader to form a conception of what the more powerful Babylonian gods were believed to be like. We have seen Anu administering the powers of heaven, we have seen Bēl upon the earth destroying mankind in his anger and directing the oracles of all the gods, and Ea in the Deep regulating the affairs of his own household and revealing secrets by his hidden wisdom. Shamash, the Sun-god, has been seen in his character as the just judge of the whole earth, hearing the appeals of such as had suffered wrong, and giving help and advice to those who needed it. The great goddess Ishtar has been revealed in two characters. She has appeared as a cruel and wanton lover, persecuting those who yielded to her passion and seeking revenge upon those who refused her love; she has also been seen in her gentler character as a devoted wife, descending to the underworld to seek her husband. Other deities have also been described in the exercise of their own peculiar functions, especially Marduk, the city-god of Babylon, who appears as the leader and the champion of the gods when they are in distress.

In addition to these greater gods many other deities, of less power and importance, have been incidentally mentioned in the course of the legends. These, however, scarcely give an adequate idea of the number of supernatural beings who were believed to exist in the heavens and upon the earth, and beneath the earth. The legends that have been described are chiefly concerned with the doings of the more powerful gods and the great heroes of antiquity, and they naturally do not deal with the sprites, and goblins, and spectres, which were believed to haunt and harass a man in his daily life and in the performance of his ordinary duties. For the ancient Babylonian moved in a world peopled by demons and spirits, whom he could not see, but whose influence at any moment might cause him misfortune, sickness, or death. Many of these spirits were actively hostile to man and waged an incessant warfare against him. Others, though less actively hostile, were to be no less feared, for at any time a man might unwittingly incur their wrath by some act which trenched upon their jealously guarded rights. An ill-omened word, or the eating or drinking of an impure thing, was sufficient to rouse the wrath of some one of these beings; and, although the victim might have committed no intentional act of disobedience, he had to endure their persecution, sometimes without even a knowledge of its cause. These beings were conceived to be of hideous and repulsive appearance, often uniting in strange combinations the bodies and limbs of various birds and beasts. The accompanying illustration is a specimen of an evil Babylonian demon, taken from a clay figure in the British Museum. The head of the monster was no doubt partly suggested by that of a lion, and its ferocious aspect betokens ill to the man who might have the misfortune to place himself within its power.

In order to realize the great number and variety of such beings it would be necessary to turn to the spells and incantations and magical formulæ which occupy so large a place in the religious literature of the Babylonians. To ignore this lower aspect of the belief of the Babylonians would be to give a one-sided and incomplete picture of their religion, but Babylonian magic does not fall within the limits of the present volume. We are here concerned with the higher side of the Babylonian religion, and, having already described the general character of the greater gods, it now remains to enquire in what relation man stood to these great deities, and also to what extent his religious beliefs affected his duty to his fellow man.

A Babylonian demon. (British Museum, No. 22,458.)

It has already been stated that, so far as we can see from their religious literature, the Babylonians had no conception of a single supreme and all-powerful God. In this matter they did not resemble the ancient Egyptians, who believed that such a being existed above the company of the gods and on a different plane from them. The Egyptian held that this all-powerful God could manifest his might in the persons of the gods of various departments of nature, but at the same time they believed that he was the ultimate cause of the entire universe and was the creator and director of both gods and men.[1] The Babylonians knew no such supreme deity, but it should be added that some few passages in their inscriptions perhaps indicate a glimmering belief in that direction.

The Babylonian word for "god" is *ilu*, and the ideograph for the word is always placed as a determinative particle before the names of deities. One of its most common uses is in the plural, in the phrase *ilâni rabûti*, "the great gods," an expression which denotes the company of the great gods as distinguished from the host of lesser deities and spirits. When *ilu* occurs in the singular it is usually in the course of the description of some particular deity, as in the phrases *ilu rabû*, "a great god," and *ilu ali-ia*, "god "of my city," applied to the god Marduk. In other passages it takes a pronominal suffix, as in the phrases

[1] See Budge, *Egyptian Ideas of the Future Life*, chap. I.

ili-ia, "my god," *ili-ka,* "thy god"; or it is coupled with the substantive *ishtar,* "goddess"; and in both these cases it is clear that the reference is made to some particular deity. There are, however, a few passages in which *ilu* stands entirely by itself, and where it is possible that it should be translated as "god" without any qualifying phrase. Such a passage occurs towards the end of the poem of the ancient king of Cuthah, which has been described in Chapter III.[1] Here the king, after narrating his own history, proceeds to offer advice to any future ruler, and he addresses his words to any "king, or ruler, or prince, "or any one whatsoever, whom the god shall call to rule "over the kingdom." No particular god is mentioned, and *ilu* occurs entirely by itself; it is possible, however, to refer the phrase to Nergal, the god of Cuthah, in whose temple the legend is preserved. In any case, this use of *ilu* is of rare occurrence, and it would be rash to rely on this evidence alone for proving that the Babylonians conceived an abstract and supreme deity apart from the separate and distinct gods of the various divisions of the natural world. Perhaps the Assyrians approached nearer to such a conception than the Babylonians, for their god Ashur was the symbol of their own national existence, and, although they retained the worship of the other gods from the Babylonians, they assigned to Ashur a position of supremacy

[1] See above p. 95.

among them and ascribed to him many of the attributes which belonged properly to the older gods.

Among the Babylonians the god Marduk in the course of time acquired a position of peculiar interest. As the god of Babylon he was naturally from the first of easy access to the inhabitants of his own city, and this intimacy with his own people was gradually extended until we find him appearing before his father Ea in the character of mediator and intercessor on behalf of men. We have already seen how Marduk was regarded as the creator of the world and of mankind, and it is in accordance with this tradition that he should have been thought to use his influence on behalf of the creatures whom he had made. Marduk's character as intercessor is well illustrated by the following extract from a religious text, the recital of which would procure relief for a sick man and remove the evil spell by which he was troubled. The text reads—

"An evil curse like a demon has beset the man,
"Sorrow and trouble have fallen upon him,
"Evil sorrow has fallen upon him,
"An evil curse, a spell, a sickness.
"The evil curse has slain that man like a lamb.
"His god has departed from his body,
"His guardian goddess has left his side.
"He is covered by sorrow and trouble as with a garment, and he is overwhelmed;

"Then Marduk beheld him,
"And he entered into the house of his father Ea and he said unto him:
"'O my father, an evil curse like a demon has beset the man.'
"Twice he spake unto him, (and he added):
"'I know not what that man has done, nor whereby he may be cured.'
"And Ea made answer to his son, Marduk, (saying):
"'O my son, what dost thou not know? what can I tell thee more?
"O Marduk, what dost thou not know? what can I tell thee more?
"What I know, thou also knowest.
"Go, my son, Marduk,
"Take him to the house of purification,
"Dissolve the spell from upon him, remove the spell from upon him.'"

The prominent position of Marduk in the company of the gods is amply attested in the numerous hymns and prayers that have been found addressed to him. Prayers and hymns, however, of a very similar nature were addressed to the other great gods, and these were believed to detract in no way from the deference due to Marduk or to any other deity. It seems to be clear that each god, when worshipped in his own temple, was regarded with profound reverence and could even be credited with sovereign power over the other gods

A MAN'S OWN GOD AND GODDESS.

without exciting their jealousy, and without laying his worshippers open to rebuke.

In the description of the sick man's evil plight, quoted above, two lines occur in which it is stated that "his "god has departed from his body, his guardian goddess "has left his side." The explanation of these two lines brings us to what is perhaps the most interesting, and at the same time the most characteristic, feature of the relationship which existed between the ancient Babylonian and his god. We have seen that Marduk appears in general as the protector and the friend of mankind, but every Babylonian had in addition two divine protectors, with whom his fortunes were most intimately connected. Each man had his own patron god and goddess, who made his welfare their peculiar charge, and to whose service he was specially devoted. In any trouble or affliction he would first turn to these two deities and implore them to exert their influence on his behalf. The mere fact that he had fallen into adversity, however, was often proof that his god and goddess were temporarily estranged, and, should this be the case, it was necessary for him first to pacify their wrath and then to secure their assistance. What principles actuated the Babylonians in their choice of patron deities are not clearly indicated in their religious literature. It is not unreasonable to suppose that a child's parents dedicated it at its birth to the care of some god and goddess, and that the choice was left entirely to them. We may be sure that whatever deities were selected they were among those who had temples or shrines in the city in which the parents lived, and who would therefore be in a position to effectually protect their offspring. The belief in guardian deities is intimately connected with the magical side of Babylonian religion, and the pacification of a man's angry god and goddess was one of the commonest objects to which spells and incantations were applied. It may be inferred therefore that the belief in these protecting gods goes back to a remote period in Babylonian history. In his combat with the invisible demons and spirits in the midst of which a man was believed to live it would have gone hard with him if he had been left to his own unaided efforts. His natural protectors were his own patron god and goddess, and he was sure of their constant care and protection, if he did nothing to offend them or estrange them from him.

When misfortune or sickness fell upon a man and he perceived that his patron deities were offended with him, his first act was to hasten to the temple of his god and goddess and secure the services of a priest who might aid him in regaining their favour. The design most frequently engraved upon Babylonian and Assyrian cylinder-seals is a representation of the owner of the seal being led by a priest into the presence of his god; and it is clear that the priest's mediation was necessary in order that the offended deity might be duly appeased.

PRIESTLY MEDIATION. 211

Frequently upon the seals an attendant is represented walking behind the owner and bearing offerings into the temple, and, when these had been handed over to the priest, the penitent was ready to be led into the god's presence. The priest then took him by the hand and both priest and penitent raised their other hands as a symbol of worship and supplication. In this order the man was led into the presence of his offended god. If he was sore afflicted with disease, or oppressed by his sense of guilt, he would sit or lie upon the ground, and with bitter sighs and groans would declare his sin and pray for absolution. Among the religious works of the Babylonians and Assyrians a number of tablets have been found which served as service-books for the use of priest and penitent when they had entered the presence of the offended deity.[1] In these service-books the priest sometimes addresses the god and describes the sad condition of the man who wishes to make his confession; at other times the penitent himself takes up the prayer. The following is an extract from one of these compositions :—

The priest: "In sorrow there he sits; With[2] cries " of affliction, in trouble of heart. With bitter tears " in bitter sorrow, Like the doves he moans grievously, " night and day. Unto his merciful god, like a wild cow,

---

[1] Cf. Zimmern, *Babylonische Busspsalmen*, Leipzig, 1885.
[2] In this and the following extracts the capital letter marks the beginning of a new line in the text.

"he cries, He makes a grievous sighing. Before his god
"he casts down his face in supplication, He weeps,
"that he may approach, that nothing may hold him
"back."

The penitent: "My deed will I declare, my
"deed which cannot be declared. My words will I
"repeat, my words which cannot be repeated. O my
"god, my deed will I declare, my deed which cannot be
"declared."

In another prayer a penitent addresses his god and
goddess together, and prays to be purified from his sin
in the following words:—

"O my god, who art angry, accept my prayer. O my
"goddess, who art angry, receive my supplication.
"Receive my supplication and let thy spirit be at rest.
"O my goddess, look with pity on me and accept my
"supplication. Let my sins be forgiven, let my trans-
"gressions be blotted out. Let the ban be torn away,
"let the bonds be loosened. Let the seven winds carry
"away my sighs. I will rend away my wickedness,
"let the bird bear it to the heavens. Let the fish carry
"off my misery, let the river sweep it away. Let the
"beast of the field take it from me. Let the flowing
"waters of the river wash me clean."

Sometimes the god or goddess to whom the prayer is
addressed is mentioned by name, as in the following
extract, in which the penitent submits himself entirely
to the will of the goddess Ishtar and seeks to arouse her

pity by a reference to his condition of abject misery. He makes his appeal to the goddess as follows :—

"O mother of the gods, who fulfils their commands, "O lady of mankind, who makes the green herb to "spring up, Who created all things, who guides the "whole of creation, O mother Ishtar, whose side no "god can approach, O exalted lady, whose command "is mighty, A prayer will I utter. That which appears "good unto her, may she do unto me! O my lady, "from the days of my youth I have been much yoked "to misfortune. Food have I not eaten, weeping was "my nourishment. Water have I not drunk, tears "were my drink. My heart never rejoices, my spirit "is never glad."

A man's appeal to his god and goddess was not always successful, for his sin may have been so great that his petitions for forgiveness were not sufficient in themselves to appease their wrath. In such a case, when the penitent found that his appeals remained unanswered, he had recourse to some more powerful god or goddess by whose assistance he sought to bring about his reconciliation with his patron deities. The following is an extract from a service-book which was intended for the use of priest and penitent upon such an occasion :—

The penitent: " I, thy servant, full of sighs, cry unto "thee. Whosoever has sinned, thou acceptest his "fervent prayer. The man on whom thou lookest in "pity, that man lives, O ruler of all things, lady of "mankind, O merciful one, whose turning is propitious, "who acceptest supplication."

The priest: "Since his god and his goddess are "angry with him, he cries unto thee. Turn to him "thy countenance and take his hand."

The penitent: "Beside thee there is no deity who "guides aright. In justice look on me with pity "and accept my supplication. Declare my forgiveness "and let thy spirit be appeased. When, O my lady, "will thy countenance be turned? I moan like the "doves, I satiate myself with sighs."

The priest: "With pain and grief his spirit is "oppressed. He sheds tears, he utters cries of woe."

It happened sometimes that a man through his transgressions offended some powerful deity, while he still retained the help and sympathy of his own god and goddess. In such a case he made his appeal at the shrine of the deity he had offended, and he believed that his own god and goddess made intercession for him at his side. The following extract is taken from a prayer to be delivered by a man who had offended Shamash the Sun-god and his wife Ai, and who sought to appease their wrath, while his own god and goddess added their voice to his appeal. The priest first described the man's humility and grief; the extract reads as follows:—

The priest: "By his face, which through tears he

"does not raise, he makes lamentation to thee. By
" his feet, on which fetters are set, he makes lamentation
" to thee. By his hand, which is spent through weari-
" ness, he makes lamentation to thee. By his breast,
" which utters cries as of a flute, he makes lamentation
" to thee."

The Penitent: " O lady, through bitterness of heart
" I cry to thee in sorrow: Declare my forgiveness. O
" lady, say to thy servant, 'It is enough.' Let thy heart
" be appeased. Bestow mercy on thy servant who is
" in affliction. Turn thy countenance towards him,
" accept his supplication. Turn in mercy towards thy
" servant, with whom thou wast angry. O lady, my
" hands are bound, I prostrate (?) myself before thee.
" Intercede for me before the mighty hero, Shamash,
" thy beloved spouse, That for a life of many days
" I may walk before thee. My god has prayed to
" thee, that thy heart may be at rest; My goddess has
" made supplication to thee, that thy spirit may be
" appeased."

A penitent usually trusted to his condition of grief and misery to move the pity of an angry god or goddess. Sometimes, however, the priest would make a reference to the offerings which the penitent would make, when he was pardoned and restored to health and prosperity. Such an inducement to pardon a penitent is urged by a priest upon an angry god in the following extract:—

"Open his bonds, remove his fetters. Make bright "his countenance, commend him to his god, his creator. "Give thy servant life, that he may praise thy power, "That he may bow down before thy greatness in all "dwellings. Receive his gift, accept his purchase-"money, That he may walk before thee in a land of "peace, That with overflowing abundance he may fill "thy shrine, That in thy temple his offerings may be "set, That with oil as with water he may anoint thy "bolts, And that with oil in abundance he may make "thy threshold overflow."

No doubt in the early periods of their religious development, the offences which the Babylonian committed were of a formal and ceremonial character. Their sufferings might be due to the infringement of a religious ordinance, or to the eating or drinking of an impure thing, or to an ill-omened word or action. There is no doubt, however, that in the course of time moral considerations tinged their earlier beliefs. Misfortune was still believed to be the result of sin and transgression, but the character of the sin was gradually changed. Injustice and evil-doing were believed to anger a man's god as much as offences against his own peculiar rites, and in this way a man's duty towards his god led to a conception of the duty he owed towards his fellow man. The belief that oppression and injustice were followed by material misfortune is well attested in a document from

Ashur-bāni-pal's library, which contains a number of warnings to a king against injustice, and which unequivocally states that any act of that description would recoil upon himself or upon his land.[1] The beginning of this tablet reads as follows :—

"If the king does not give heed to justice, his people "shall be overthrown and his land shall be brought to "confusion.

"If he gives no heed to the law of his land, Ea, the "king of destinies, shall change his destiny, and shall "visit him with misfortune.

"If he gives no heed to his nobles, his days shall "(not) be long.

"If he gives no heed to the wise-men, his land shall "revolt against him.

"If he gives heed to wisdom (?), the king shall behold "the strengthening of the land.

"If he gives heed to the commands of Ea, the great "gods shall endow him with true knowledge and dis- "cernment.

"If he treats a man of Sippar with injustice and "gives a harsh decision, Shamash, the judge of heaven "and earth, shall give a harsh decision in his land, "and shall appoint a just prince and a just judge in "place of injustice.

"If the men of Nippur come to him for judgment

[1] The text is published in *Cuneiform Inscriptions of Western Asia*, Vol. IV., pl. 48.

218 A MAN'S DUTIES TO HIS NEIGHBOUR.

"and he accepts gifts and treats them with injustice,
"Bēl, the lord of the world, shall bring a foreign foe
"against him and shall overthrow his army, and his
"prince and his leader they shall hunt as outcasts (?)
"through the streets.

"If the men of Babylon take money with them and
"give bribes, and he favours the cause of (these)
"Babylonians and turns to (their) entreaty, Marduk,
"the lord of heaven and earth, shall bring his foe
"against him, and shall give his goods and his posses-
"sions to his enemy. And the men of Nippur, Sippar,
"or Babylon who do these things shall be cast into
"prison."

In this tablet it is clearly stated that the gods would punish oppression and injustice with misfortune, and there is evidence of this belief in other Babylonian documents of a religious nature. From a series of magical incantations we learn that a wrong committed by a man against his neighbour carried with it a punishment no less severe than that which accompanied any offence against a ceremonial code.[1] The various sins which a man might commit are enumerated in the form of questions, and the following extract will serve to indicate their general character:—

"Has he estranged the father from his son? Has
"he estranged the son from his father? Has he
"estranged the mother from her daughter? Has he

[1] Cf. Zimmern, *Die Beschwörungstafeln Schurpu*, pp. 3 ff.

"estranged the daughter from her mother? Has
"he estranged the mother-in-law from her daughter-
"in-law? Has he estranged the daughter-in-law
"from her mother-in-law? Has he estranged the
"brother from his brother? Has he estranged the
"friend from his friend? Has he estranged the com-
"panion from his companion? Has he refused to set
"a captive free, or has he refused to loose one who
"was bound? Has he shut out a prisoner from the
"light? Has he said of a captive 'Hold him fast,'
"or of one who was bound has he said, 'Strengthen
"his bonds?' Has he committed a sin against a god,
"or has he committed a sin against a goddess? Has
"he offended a god, or has he held a goddess in light
"esteem? Is his sin against his own god, or is his
"sin against his own goddess? Has he done violence
"to one older than himself, or has he conceived
"hatred against an elder brother? Has he held his
"father and mother in contempt, or has he insulted his
"elder sister? Has he been generous in small things,
"but avaricious in great matters? Has he said 'yea'
"for 'nay'? Has he said 'nay' for 'yea'? Has he
"spoken of unclean things, or [has he counselled] dis-
"obedience? Has he uttered wickedness? . . . Has
"he used false scales? . . . Has he accepted a wrong
"account, or has he refused a rightful sum? Has
"he disinherited a legitimate son, or has he recognized
"an illegitimate son? Has he set up a false landmark,

"or has he refused to set up a true landmark? Has "he removed bound, border, or landmark? Has he "broken into his neighbour's house? Has he drawn "near his neighbour's wife? Has he shed his neigh- "bour's blood? Has he stolen his neighbour's gar- "ment?"

Here we have enumerated a comprehensive series of sins and offences, the commission of any one of which was considered sufficient to bring down upon a man the wrath of his god. Taken together they prove that in the seventh century before Christ, if not earlier, the Babylonians and Assyrians possessed a system of morality which in many respects resembled that of the descendants of Abraham.

THE END.

PRINTED BY WILLIAM CLOWES AND SONS, LIMITED, LONDON AND BECCLES.

www.ingramcontent.com/pod-product-compliance
Lightning Source LLC
Chambersburg PA
CBHW021810230426
43669CB00008B/705